English Connections

GRAMMAR FOR COMMUNICATION

BOOK 2

LINDA LEE

Project Editor
Marietta Urban

CONTEMPORARY BOOKS

a division of NTC/CONTEMPORARY PUBLISHING GROUP
Lincolnwood, Illinois USA

Library of Congress Cataloging-in-Publication Data

English connections.
      Cover title: Contemporary's English connections.
      Bk. 1 has statement of responsibility: Isabel
Kentengian ; bk. 2: Linda Lee.
      1. English language—Textbooks for foreign speakers.
I. Kentengian, Isabel.   II. Lee, Linda, 1950–
III. Title: Contemporary's English connections.
PE1128.L42   1993   428.2′4   93-22804
ISBN 0-8092-4205-2 (bk. 1 : pbk.)
ISBN 0-8092-4206-0 (bk. 2)

Story "Christmas in Mexico," by Soraya Silas, on page 29
reprinted by permission of the author.

Story "An Important Event in My Life," by James St. Fleur, on
page 59 reprinted by permission of the author.

Bulgarian joke on page 104 from *Laughing Together*, by
Barbara K. Walker. Copyright © 1992 by Free Spirit
Publishing, Inc., Minneapolis, MN. Reprinted by permission of
Free Spirit Publishing, Inc. All rights reserved.

Poem "My Rules," on page 144, from *Where the Sidewalk
Ends*, by Shel Silverstein. Copyright © 1974 by Evil Eye
Music, Inc. Selection reprinted by permission of HarperCollins
Publishers.

ISBN: 0-8092-4206-0

Published by Contemporary Books,
a division of NTC/Contemporary Publishing Group,
4255 West Touhy Avenue,
Lincolnwood (Chicago), Illinois 60646-1975 U.S.A.
© 1994 by Linda Lee

8 9 0 GB(H)) 10 9 8 7 6 5

Editorial Director	*Illustrator*
Mark Boone	Linda Reilly
Editorial	*Line Art*
Charlotte Ullman	William Colrus
Eunice Hoshizaki	Jeff Weyer
Michael O'Neill	
	Art & Production
Editorial Assistant	Jan Geist
Maggie McCann	Sue Springston
Editorial Production Manager	*Typography*
Norma Underwood	Ellen Kollmon
Production Editor	*Cover Photograph*
Thomas D. Scharf	© David W. Hamilton
	The Image Bank
Cover Design	
Georgene Sainati	Special thanks to Caren Van Slyke

Contents

Acknowledgments

Diane Larsen-Freeman
Chief Consultant
Master of Arts in Teaching (MAT) Program
School for International Training, Brattleboro, Vermont

Judy Hanlon, Oxnard Adult School, Oxnard, California

Renee Klosz, Lindsey Hopkins Technical Education Center, Miami, Florida

Suzanne Leibman, College of Lake County, Grayslake, Illinois

Fatiha Makloufi, Community Development Agency, New York, New York

Sharon O'Malley, Region IV Educational Service Center, Houston, Texas

Catherine Porter, Adult Education Service Center, Des Plaines, Illinois

Betsy Rubin, Chicago, Illinois

Introduction

English Connections: Grammar for Communication is a three-level series for beginning to low-intermediate adult learners of English as a second language. It integrates a developmental grammar syllabus with real-life contexts within the framework of the communicative approach to language teaching.

The goal of this series is to help language learners use grammar accurately, meaningfully, and appropriately so that they can communicate effectively outside the classroom.

The inspiration behind *English Connections* is Diane Larsen-Freeman's framework for teaching grammar. It focuses on the three dimensions of grammar: form, meaning, and use. All three dimensions are equally important. Throughout this series, information on form, meaning, and use is presented whenever appropriate.

Grammar points that naturally occur together are presented and practiced within meaningful contexts through activities that are student-centered and highly interactive. Useful vocabulary relating to the contexts is also integrated into the lessons. The purpose of this series is to encourage grammatical accuracy within useful contexts that promote real communication in English. This is grammar for communication.

The Form / Meaning / Use Framework of *English Connections*

This series pushes beyond a focus on form to include the dimensions of meaning and use as well. What do we mean by these terms? Let's look at an example from Book 2. Modals such as *should, could,* and *had better* are introduced in Unit 14.

How are modals formed?

The form of the modals *should, could,* and *had better* is described visually in a paradigm in the grammar boxes. (For example, *Rita should work in a clothing store. She could work longer hours. She had better go to the doctor.*) Most verbs change form in the third person singular present tense; however, modals always have the same form. Also, *to* is not added before the main verb.

What do these modals mean?

Should, could, and *had better* are grouped together in Unit 14 in appropriate contexts to help clarify their meaning. *Should* is used for advice when there appears to be only one solution to a problem. (*Rita should work in a clothing store.*) *Could* is used for suggestions, especially when there are two or more possible solutions to a problem. (*Rita wants to earn more money. What should she do? She could work longer hours.* OR: *She could get a second job.*) *Had better* is used for even more urgent advice (*Rita has a fever of 104°F. She had better go to the doctor*).

When are these modals used?

The difference in authority levels between speakers influences the choice of which modal to use. A friend talking to a sick friend might say, *You should stay in bed today*, whereas a supervisor speaking to an employee would probably choose the more urgent form: *You had better come to work today!*

From this example we can see that teaching a grammar point involves teaching not only the form but the meaning and use as well. Information on form, meaning, and use for each grammar point is provided in detail in *English Connections Book 2, Teacher's Edition*, especially in the Grammar Guide page that precedes the step-by-step teaching suggestions for each unit.

Learning a Second Language

People learn a second language in many different ways. For example, visual learners learn best by looking at graphic representations of concepts. Auditory learners learn best by listening to explanations. Kinesthetic/tactile learners learn best by manipulating objects and moving around.

English Connections addresses a variety of learning styles. For example, graphic icons represent directions to visual learners, and there are grammar boxes designed to aid these learners as well. Listening exercises along with pair and small-group activities encourage auditory learners. Total Physical Response (TPR) activities appeal to kinesthetic/tactile learners.

Language learning is a gradual process, and people learn about form, meaning, and use little by little. In *English Connections*, only one part of a grammar point is presented at a time. More information about form, meaning, and use unfolds as learners gain familiarity with grammar points, which are recycled for continuous practice. Finally, review units provide practice in freer, less-structured real-life contexts.

About the Series

English Connections: Grammar for Communication consists of:

- Three student books
- Three teacher's editions
- Three workbooks
- Two audiocassettes for each level of the series

Each student book has fifteen units, five review units, a teacher script for listening exercises, an appendix with mini-exercises, and an answer key.

Each teacher's edition includes a detailed scope-and-sequence chart and full-page representations from the student book with cues for the workbook. Each unit contains a Grammar Guide page with useful background information about each grammar point, step-by-step teaching suggestions, extension activities, and a complete answer key.

Each workbook provides extended focused practice for grammar and vocabulary from each unit in the student book.

The audiocassettes include all listening exercises (also in the teacher script), all dialogues other than writing exercises, and most of the Connections and Small Talk sections.

Teaching *English Connections*

Gray bars are used in each unit to signal a logical stopping point in the text. This feature can be useful in planning classroom time, since you will not be able to complete an entire unit in one class period.

All four language skills (Listening, Speaking, Reading, and Writing) are integrated from the very beginning in Unit One. To identify the language skills that are practiced in each exercise, graphic symbols are used as pre-reading cues. Many times they are used in combination, since more than one skill is practiced at a time.

The following notes describe the recurring features in the student book.

Opening Illustrations

Each unit opens with an illustration that provides a natural setting for the grammar points and vocabulary of the unit.

Elicit from students as much language as you can about the picture. Ask questions about the people and encourage students to guess what is happening.

Setting the Scene

This regular feature consists of a short conversation using authentic language that provides a context for the grammar points of the unit.

Introduce the characters in the conversation. Then read the conversation aloud a few times as naturally as possible. Have students practice it in pairs and listen to them practice.

Their pronunciation may not be perfect at this time. Don't correct every mistake you hear—this may cause students to become hesitant to speak English. Instead, write down one or two common mistakes that you may hear. Then tell the class as a group to repeat the correct pronunciation after you and encourage accuracy on those points.

Grammar Boxes

Grammatical terms are kept to a minimum throughout *English Connections*. The grammar boxes include many examples, and students are encouraged to guess the rule.

Choose examples from the box and write them on the board. Elicit more examples from the students. After giving many examples, elicit the rule from the students or, if necessary, present it in your own words. After presenting the grammar point orally, use the grammar box as a summary of the form/meaning/use information. (The teacher's editions provide step-by-step teaching suggestions for presenting each grammar point.)

The presentation of each grammar point is followed by a combination of focused and communicative practice. The goal is to help students learn to use the grammar for communication.

Focus on Vocabulary

The most effective way to learn grammar is in a meaningful context. To develop a meaningful context, relevant vocabulary is introduced. Vocabulary boxes are interspersed throughout each unit as the contexts require.

Bring in realia (real objects) or draw pictures on the board to illustrate words. Ask questions using the words in the box. Have students actively work with new vocabulary (for example, by categorizing, comparing, or contrasting words or ideas).

Small Talk

This feature presents a natural conversation that incorporates a grammar point from the unit and is followed by an exercise or an activity that allows students to practice the language.

Model the conversation with a more advanced student.

Partnerwork

This feature is a two-page information-gap activity. Students work together in pairs. Each person has information that his or her partner does not have, and each person should look at his or her own page only. Students work together to obtain the information orally from their partners to complete their task. As with all pair and small-group activities, it will get a little noisy. Don't worry—a lot of meaningful language learning is taking place!

Try to pair more advanced students with those who need extra practice. Have pairs of students compare their answers in a class session.

Use What You Know

This feature is a communicative activity that involves all four skills (listening, speaking, reading, and writing) and is based on a context from the unit.

In Your Own Words

This feature provides an opportunity for more communicative practice. Students work in pairs or small groups to complete an oral and/or written task involving their own personal information.

Wrapping Up

The final feature of the unit, Wrapping Up provides a summary practice with the most important grammar points presented in the unit.

Review Units

Periodic Review Units provide opportunities for freer, more communicative practice. Review Units are cumulative, and present previously introduced grammar points in interesting new contexts. Learner-generated stories are included that describe holidays in students' countries and important events in students' lives.

Teacher Script for Listening Exercises

Some grammar points are hard to distinguish in normal conversation. ("Was it singular or plural? Was it present or past tense?") Several listening exercises are included that relate to the grammar points presented. Students are asked to listen to the teacher and mark the answer that they hear. Once students can hear the difference between singular and plural or between past and present, it will be easier for them to say the difference.

Listening Exercises are preceded by listening and writing icons. Refer to the Teacher Script pages 145–147. Be sure to read the teacher script as naturally as possible, allowing for the particular needs of your students.

Appendix

The Appendix provides detailed information along with mini-exercises on pronunciation and spelling of selected grammar points. It also includes useful vocabulary, such as common first and last names in the United States, weights and measures, and two-word verbs. See the *Book 2 Teacher's Edition* for information on when and how to present the material.

Answer Key

Answers for all written exercises are provided in the Answer Key beginning on page 172. Each teacher's edition includes a complete answer key for all the exercises in the corresponding student book.

Successful Language Learning

Language learning is enhanced when students are actively and cheerfully engaged in the learning process. Sometimes students may prefer not to offer personal information about themselves. Sensitivity to their feelings is the best guide. Let students know that they can use fictitious information if they prefer.

The most important factor for success is to create a classroom atmosphere in which learning is enjoyable and relatively stress free, so students feel safe yet challenged. Happy teaching!

> Look for grammar-guide pages, step-by-step teaching suggestions, and extension activities in *English Connections Book 2, Teacher's Edition*.

◆ Simple Present
  (Statements)
  (Negative Statements)
  (Yes/No Questions and Short
  Answers)
◆ Adverbs of Frequency
◆ *Wh*-Question: *When*

Unit 1   What do you do every day?

These are things Ramón does every day. What do you do every day?

Setting the Scene

David: Do you cook dinner every day, Mr. Sánchez?
Ramón: Well, I usually do.
David: I don't believe it!
Ramón: Why not?
David: Because my father never cooks dinner.

Simple Present (Statements)

Ramón works every day.

I You We They	**work**	every day.		He She It	**works**	every day.

Use the simple present when you talk about things you do as a habit.

Look at the Appendix on page 148 for spelling rules.

1 What do you do every day? Write four activities.

1. *I eat breakfast every day.* _____

2. _____

3. _____

4. _____

5. _____

2 Read a classmate's list. Tell the class what your classmate does every day.

Example: *1. Jules eats breakfast every day.*
2. He reads the newspaper every day.
3. He goes to school every day.
4. He works every day.
5. He studies every day.

Simple Present (Negative Statements)

Ramón doesn't work on Saturday.
The bird doesn't sing at night.

I	**don't**	work on Saturday.	She	**doesn't**	work on Saturday.
You			He		
We					
They					

The bird	**doesn't**	sing at night.
It		

The contractions *don't* and *doesn't* are used mostly in speaking and informal situations.

Contractions:
do not
↓
don't

does not
↓
doesn't

3 **Listen to your teacher. What does Fariba do on Saturday? Circle YES or NO.**

1. She gets up early.   YES   NO

2. She works on Saturday.   YES   NO

3. She goes to school.   (YES) NO

4. She studies English.   YES (NO)

5. She goes shopping.   YES (NO)

4 **Many people don't work on the weekend. Children don't go to school on the weekend. How is the weekend special for you?**

1. ____I don't get up early.____

2. ____I go shopping.____

3. ____I go shopping____

4. ____I go to church____

5. ____I goin vist at may fread's____

5 **Read a classmate's list for Exercise 4. Tell about your classmate.**

Example: *Sylvia doesn't get up early on Saturday.*
She goes shopping.

Simple Present (Yes/No Questions and Short Answers)

Do	you I we they	work every day?	Yes,	I you we they	do.	No,	I you we they	don't.
Does	she he			she he	does.		she he	doesn't.
Does	the bird	sing every day?		it			it	

6 **Find out about a classmate's daily activities. Check YES or NO. Add three more activities.**

A: Do you *go to school* every day?

B: Yes, I do. OR No, I don't.

	YES	NO
1. go to school	✓	✓
2. get up early		
3. watch TV	✓	
4. go to work		✓
5. drink coffee		✓
6. exercise		✓
7. *drive a car*	✓	
8. *walking*		✓
9. *restaurant*		✓

7 **Find someone in the class who *speaks Spanish*. Get his or her signature. Do the same for 2-7.**

A: Do you *speak Spanish*?

B: Yes, I do. OR No, I don't.

Signature

1. speaks Spanish   *Carmen*

2. has two children   *Carmen Luno*

3. likes coffee   *Moreno*

4. has a brother   *Sergio*

5. lives near school   *Yolanda*

6. has a pet   *Luhli Cyl*

7. *has gold car*   *Jose Franco*

Adverbs of Frequency

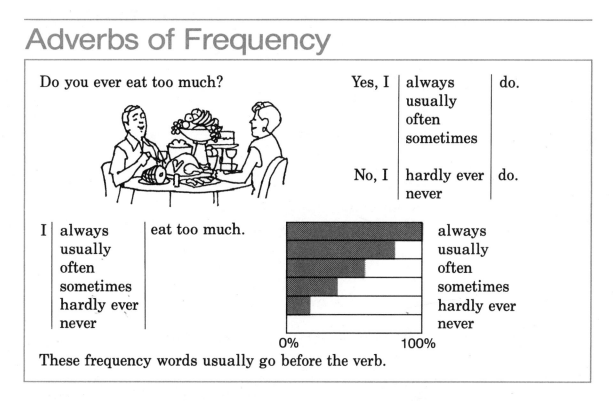

Do you ever eat too much?

Yes, I	always usually often sometimes	do.
No, I	hardly ever never	do.

I	always usually often sometimes hardly ever never	eat too much.

always
usually
often
sometimes
hardly ever
never

0%   100%

These frequency words usually go before the verb.

8   Ask a partner the following questions. Check *always, usually, often, sometimes, hardly ever*, or *never*.

A: Do you ever *drive to school*?
B: *No, I never do.*

	always	usually	often	sometimes	hardly ever	never
drive to school	✓					✓
take the bus to school						✓
miss the bus					✓	✓
walk to school						
speak English at home	✓					
get up early				✓		
sleep late				✓		
clean car						
drive work every day	✓			✓		
shopping every day						

9   Now tell the class about your partner.

Example: *Maria never drives to school.*
         She usually takes the bus to school.

Wh-Question: *When*

When	do	you they	usually get up?	At 6:30.
	does	he she		At 7:00.

10 **When do you usually do the following activities? Put them into three groups. Share your answers with a partner.**

eat a big meal   talk to friends   eat breakfast

go shopping   watch TV   read the paper

in the morning	in the afternoon	in the evening
eat breakfast		

Focus on Vocabulary

Telling Time

Listen to your teacher. What time is it? Add hands to these clocks.

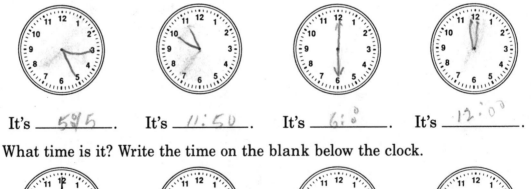

It's ___5:45___.   It's ___11:50___.   It's ___6:00___.   It's ___12:00___.

What time is it? Write the time on the blank below the clock.

_____   _____   _____   _____

What time is it now? _____

11 **Work with a partner. Take turns asking questions. Write your partner's answers on the blank lines.**

A: When do you usually *get up?*
B: At *6 o'clock.*

Activity	Time
1. eat breakfast	9:0 a m
2. leave for class	6:50 t m
3. eat dinner	8:30 t m
4. go to bed	10:30 P m
5. ~~go to work~~	7:00 A m

12 **Who gets up first in the morning? Make a class list on the board. Write the time and each person's name. Put the earliest time first.**

Example: A: When do you get up?
B: At *6:15.*
C: At *7:00.*

Partnerwork ▶ Person A

Take a trip across the U.S. Person A looks at this page only. Person B looks at page 8 only. Take turns asking questions. Fill in the information on your bus schedule.

Example: A: When does the bus *leave Cleveland?*
B: At *8:15 in the evening.*

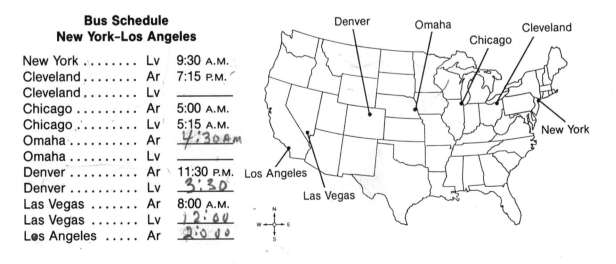

Bus Schedule
New York–Los Angeles

New York	Lv	9:30 A.M.
Cleveland	Ar	7:15 P.M.
Cleveland	Lv	
Chicago	Ar	5:00 A.M.
Chicago	Lv	5:15 A.M.
Omaha	Ar	4:30 AM
Omaha	Lv	
Denver	Ar	11:30 P.M.
Denver	Lv	3:30
Las Vegas	Ar	8:00 A.M.
Las Vegas	Lv	12:00
Los Angeles	Ar	2:000

Take a trip across the U.S. Person B looks at this page only. Person A looks at page 7 only. Take turns asking questions. Fill in the information on your bus schedule.

Example: B: When does the bus *leave New York?*
A: At *9:30 in the morning.*

Bus Schedule
New York–Los Angeles

New York	Lv	_____
Cleveland	Ar	_____
Cleveland	Lv	8:15 P.M.
Chicago	Ar	_____
Chicago	Lv	_____
Omaha	Ar	3:15 P.M.
Omaha	Lv	3:30 P.M.
Denver	Ar	_____
Denver	Lv	12:15 A.M.
Las Vegas	Ar	_____
Las Vegas	Lv	9:00 A.M.
Los Angeles	Ar	2:00 P.M.

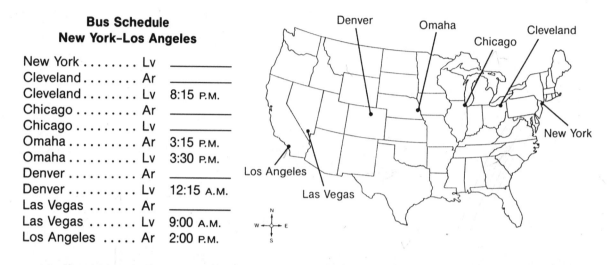

Focus on Vocabulary

Chores at Home

Do you do these chores at home?

do the dishes make the beds do the laundry

cook dinner vacuum take out the garbage

13 What chores do the people do at your home? List each person's name on a piece of paper. Then tell what chores each person does. Compare charts with a classmate. Follow this example:

Names	Activities
Me	*I usually cook. I always make the beds.*
Boris	*Boris sometimes cooks.* *He often does the laundry.*

14 Find out about a classmate. Take turns asking questions. Use checks to show your classmate's answers.

    A: Do you ever *do the dishes?*
    B: *No, I hardly ever do.*

	always	usually	often	sometimes	hardly ever	never
do the dishes						
take out the garbage						
make the beds						
do the laundry						
cook						
vacuum						

15 What does Ramón do in the morning? Number the pictures in the correct order. Then write his schedule on the next page.

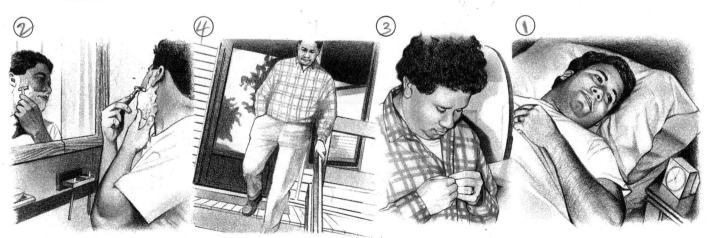

16 Write Ramón's morning schedule.

Time	Activity
6:30	1. _He wakes up._
6:45	2. _He ~~it~~ shaves._
7:00	3. _He gets dressed_
7:30	4. _He goes ~~to the~~ work_

In Your Own Words

What do you do in the morning? Write your schedule.

Time	Activity
7:00	_I get up._
7:30	_My day is ~~brushe~~ in mouch._
4:45	_the morning is Cooking louch._
8:00	_She tokin ~~bimmer~~._
5:00	

Wrapping Up

Write the words in the correct column. Use your own information.

Do you ever *cook a big meal*?

> go to the movies
>
> go to bed late
>
> get up at noon
>
> eat sushi

every day	sometimes	hardly ever	never
			cook a big meal

Now add some more activities to the chart. Compare with a classmate.

◆ Present of *Be*
◆ Present Continuous
  (Statements)
  (Negative Statements)
  (Yes/No Questions and Short
  Answers)

Unit 2   Are you busy now?

Is Maria busy? Tell a classmate what Maria is doing in each picture.

Setting the Scene

Magda:	Hi, Maria. Are you busy now?
Maria:	Well, I'm cooking dinner right now and the baby's crying. Can I call you back?
Magda:	Sure.

Present of *Be*

am		is		are	
I **am**	busy now.	Maria **is**	busy now.	We **are**	busy now.
I'**m**	busy now.	Maria'**s** She'**s** He'**s** It'**s**	busy now.	We'**re** You'**re** They'**re**	busy now.

Use the contractions of *be* (*'m, 's, 're*) in speaking and informal writing.

1 **How do you feel now? Use these words or add your own.**

tired   sad   thirsty   hungry   mad   happy   fine

1. _I'm hungry._

2. _____

3. _____

2 **Read a classmate's sentences. Tell the class about your classmate.**

Example: 1. *Anna's hungry now.*

　　　　　2. *She's _____ now.*

Present Continuous (Statements)

Maria's cooking dinner now.

am eating	**is eating**	**are eating**
I'm eating now.	He | **'s eating** now. She | It |	We | **'re eating** now. You | They |

Use the present continuous when you talk about something you are doing now.

Look at the Appendix on page 149 for spelling rules.

3   What are Maria's children doing now? Tell a classmate.

Pablo   Tina and Juanita   Carlos

4   Practice this conversation with a partner. Then look at the pictures and create your own.

Magda: Hi, Maria. Are you busy now?
Maria: Well, I'm *cooking dinner right now and the baby's crying.*
          Can I call you back?
Magda: Sure.

5   Now tell about yourself.

Your partner: Hi, _____. Are you busy now?

You: Well, I'm _____ right now. Can I call you back?

Present Continuous (Negative Statements)

am not			is not		are not
I **am not**		He	**is not**	You	**are not**
I'm not	sleeping.	He	**'s not** sleeping.	You	**'re not** sleeping.
		She	**isn't**	We	**aren't**
		It		The boys	
				They	

Both negative contractions of *is not* and *are not* are correct. The meaning is the same.

6 **Look at the picture. The sentences below are not true. Why not? Write your ideas. Then compare with a classmate.**

1. The woman is doing the dishes.
2. The man is reading.
3. The baby is talking on the telephone.
4. The boy is watching TV.
5. The girls are studying at the table.
6. The cat is sleeping.

1. _The woman isn't doing the dishes. She's vacuuming._
2. _____
3. _____
4. _____
5. _____
6. _____

Present Continuous (Yes/No Questions and Short Answers)

Are you			I am.		I'm not.
Is the baby	sleeping now?	Yes,	he is.	No,	he isn't.
Is she			she is.		she isn't.
Is it			it is.		it isn't.
Are they			they are.		they aren't.
Are we			we are.		we aren't.

Don't use contractions in short answers after *yes*.

7 **Maria is visiting her sister Rita. She calls up her husband and asks these questions. Write her husband's answers.**

1. Maria: Is the baby sleeping?
   Ramón: _No he isn't. He's eating._

2. Maria: Is Carlos studying?
   Ramón: _____

3. Maria: Are you cooking dinner?
   Ramón: _____

4. Maria: Are Tina and Juanita helping you?
   Ramón: _____

8 **Take turns asking and answering questions about Maria's family.**

Clothes for Cold and Hot Weather

Put these clothing words into two groups.

sandals	gloves	bathing suit	sweater
jacket	scarf	boots	short-sleeved shirt
shorts	coat	tank top	baseball hat

Clothes for Cold Weather

_____

_____

_____

_____

_____

_____

Clothes for Hot Weather

_____

_____

_____

_____

_____

_____

Focus on Vocabulary

Clothes for Work and Home

Put these words in two groups. Some words go in both groups.

suit	nightgown	dress	hard hat
blue jeans	T-shirt	sweatshirt	tennis shoes
uniform	bathrobe	tie	pajamas

Clothes for Work

_____

_____

_____

_____

_____

Clothes for Home

_____

_____

_____

_____

_____

9 What are these people wearing? Tell a classmate.

Example: *He's wearing a tuxedo.*

10 Think of a person in your class. Your classmates will ask you questions about the person. Answer *yes* or *no*.

Example: A:　　I'm thinking of *a man*.　　Class: *Is he tall?*
Is he wearing blue jeans?
Is he wearing a sweater?

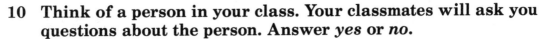

Partnerwork　　　　　　　　　　　　　▶ Person A

Work with a classmate. Person A looks at this picture only. Person B looks at the picture on page 18 only. What is different in the pictures? Take turns asking questions.

Example: A:　　*Is Maria standing up in your picture?*
B:　　*No, she isn't. She's sitting down.*

Maria　　　　　　Rita　　　　　　Philip　　　　　　Laura　　Miguel

Work with a classmate. Person B looks at this picture only. Person A looks at the picture on page 17 only. What is different in the pictures? Take turns asking questions.

Example: A: *Is Rita talking to Maria in your picture?*
B: *No, she isn't. She's talking to Philip.*

Use What You Know

Choose a magazine advertisement (ad) with people in it. Describe the people to your classmates. But don't show them the picture. Then ask your classmates, "*What is the ad for?*"

Wrapping Up

Maria sometimes sends photographs to her friend Diana. What does she write on the back of this photo? Write down your ideas on a separate sheet of paper.

This is Carlos's
birthday party. He's
seven years old. He's
sitting near the
birthday cake.

- ♦ Singular and Plural Nouns
- ♦ Count and Noncount Nouns
- ♦ *A lot of, a few/a little*
- ♦ *Some* and *any*
- ♦ Wh-Question: *How many/ How much*

Unit 3 Two pounds, please

Do you ever shop at the deli counter? What do you usually buy there?

Setting the Scene

Magda: Do you have any smoked turkey?

Deli worker: Sure. How much do you want?

Magda: About two pounds, please.

Singular and Plural Nouns

Singular (one)	Plural (two or more)
egg	eggs
lemon	lemons
dish	dishes
sandwich	sandwiches
baby	babies
lady	ladies
tomato	tomatoes
potato	potatoes
child	child**ren**
man	men
woman	women

Look at the Appendix pages 150–154 for information about syllables and for pronunciation and spelling rules.

1 Listen to your teacher. Is it singular or plural? Circle A or B.

1. A: Please bring your book to class.
   B: Please bring your books to class.

2. A: Put the dish over here.
   B: Put the dishes over here.

3. A: Write your story for tomorrow.
   B: Write your stories for tomorrow.

4. A: Ask the man for directions.
   B: Ask the men for directions.

2 Write the plural form of these words. Then say both forms.

1. pound _____
2. dish _____
3. child _____
4. woman _____

Count and Noncount Nouns

People think of **count nouns** as separate things. It is easy to count them.

1 potato   2 potatoes   3 potatoes

People think of **noncount nouns** as wholes. It is *not* easy to count them.

rice

3   Put Magda's food into two groups.

Count	Noncount

cereal

sugar

carrots

onions

tomatoes

rice

4   Think of things you find at the gas station. Then put them into two groups.

Count	Noncount
tires	air
car	gas
gas pumps	oil

A lot of, A few/A little

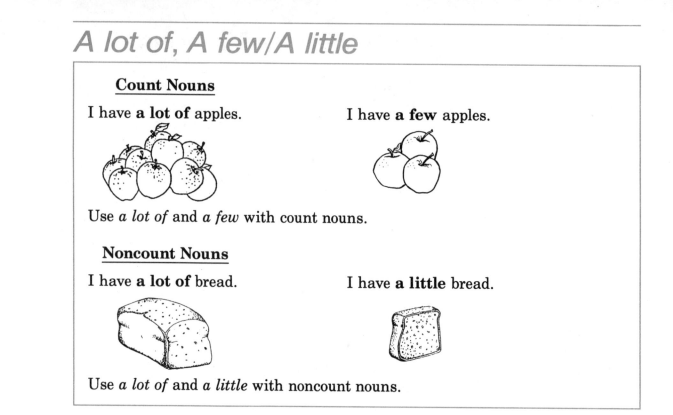

Count Nouns

I have **a lot of** apples.

I have **a few** apples.

Use *a lot of* and *a few* with count nouns.

Noncount Nouns

I have **a lot of** bread.

I have **a little** bread.

Use *a lot of* and *a little* with noncount nouns.

5 **What does Magda have in her refrigerator? Use *a lot of, a few*, or *a little*.**

a few tomatoes

a few eggs

a little milk

a little juice

a few onions

a little cheese

6 **Think of a favorite dish. What do you need for it? Make a list.**

Example:
Spaghetti with tomato sauce

a lot of spaghetti

a little garlic

a few onions

a little salt

a little cheese

name of dish

Some and Any

Count

Do you have **any** apples?
Yes, I have **some**.   No, I don't have **any**.
Yes, I do.   No, I don't.
Sure.   No, sorry.

Noncount

Do you have **any** bread?
Yes, I have **some**.   No, I don't have **any**.
Yes, I do.   No, I don't.
Sure.   No, sorry.

> You can also use *some* in a question when you are offering something: *Do you want some cake?*

7 **Read the shopping list. Play the role of the customer. Ask the deli worker for the things you need.**

Shopping List

1 pound of smoked turkey

2 pounds of salami

1 pound of provolone cheese

2 pounds of cole slaw

1 pound of green olives

1 pound of fruit salad

turkey   salami

provolone   green olives

Customer: Do you have any *smoked turkey*?
Deli worker: Sure. How much do you want?
Customer: *About a pound.*

Customer: Do you have any *cole slaw*?
Deli worker: No, sorry, we don't have *any*.

8 **Work with a partner. What does your partner have in the refrigerator at home? Make a list.**

Example: A: Do you have any *eggs*?
B: *Yes, I do.*

— _Some eggs_____

_____

_____

_____

Count	Noncount
How many quarters do you need? Just a few.	**How much** money do you need? Just a little.
How many tacos do you want? Just a few.	**How much** hot sauce do you want? Just a little.
Use *how many* with count nouns.	Use *how much* with noncount nouns.

9 Look at the pictures. Then practice this conversation.

strawberries   cookies   coffee   cake   grapes   sugar

Count

A: Do you want some *strawberries*?

B: Sure.

A: How many?

B: Just a few.

Noncount

A: Do you want some *cake*?

B: Sure.

A: How much?

B: Just a little.

mints

10 Ask a classmate. Put a check to show your classmate's answers.

How many eggs do you eat every week?

How much meat do you eat every week?

ninguno

	parte **a lot**	**a little**	**a few**	**none** **(not any)**
eggs			✓	
meat		✓		
candy			✓	
rice		✓		
junk food		✓		
apples			✓	

comida chatarra ←

Quantity Words

Quantity words make it possible to count noncount nouns.

cups   bowls   glasses

slices   teaspoons   pieces

Use this pattern: _____ _____ of _____ (**two slices of bread**)
(number)

11 **Look at this picture. What does Magda's son usually eat for breakfast?**

1. _two slices of bread_
2. _one glass of milk_
3. _one glass of juice_
4. _one bowl of cereal_

12 **What do you usually have for breakfast? Make a list. Compare with a classmate.**

Example: a glass of orange juice
two cups of coffee
a bowl of cereal with a little milk

_____

_____

_____

_____

Focus on Vocabulary

Measure Words

Measure words also make it possible to count noncount nouns. In the U.S., many people use these measure words:

½ lit.

4 quarts = 1 gallon   16 ounces = 1 pound
2 pints = 1 quart
2 cups = 1 pint

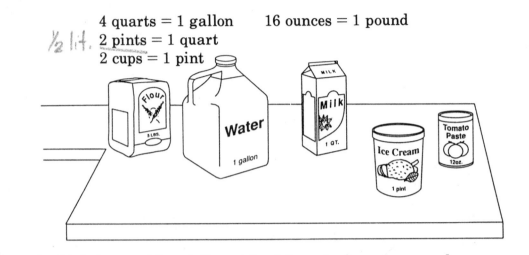

Many food labels use abbreviations (short forms) of measure words:

pound = lb.   ounce = oz.   quart = qt.

Use this pattern: **a _____ of _____.**
(**a pound of bread**)

Look at the Appendix on page 155 for a list of weights and measures.

13 Read these labels. Write the amounts. Use abbreviations.

1. ___1 pound (LB)___ of cereal
2. ___1 pound (LB)___ of sugar
3. ___1 quarts (QT)___ of milk
4. ___1 pound (LB)___ of rice
5. ___½ Gallon (gal.)___ of juice
6. ___1 pint (pt.)___ of cream
7. ___16 ounces (oz.)___ of yogurt
8. ___1 gallon (gal.)___ of water

14 How much food do you have at home? Find five containers. Tell how much food is in each container.

Example: *1 quart of milk*
1 pound of sour cream

_____

_____

_____

_____

_____

15 With several classmates, plan a meal for the class. Write your menu below. Then make a shopping list. Write how much of each food you need to prepare the meal for the class.

Menu	Shopping List	
	Quantity Word	**Food**
_____	_____	
_____	_____	
_____	_____	
_____	_____	
_____	_____	
	_____	
	_____	
	_____	

In Your Own Words

This is what you need to make nine servings of corn bread:

1¼ cups flour
¾ cup corn meal
¼ cup sugar
2 teaspoons baking powder

¼ teaspoon salt
1 egg
1 cup milk
¼ cup vegetable oil

**Think of a dish from your country. What do you need to make it?
Make a list on a piece of paper. Read your list to the class. Is it
for breakfast, lunch, or dinner? Let the class guess.**

Wrapping Up

**Put these words into two groups. Then write the plural form of
the count nouns. Compare with a classmate.**

sugar	salt	potato	juice
orange	lemon	pound	man
teaspoon	water	oil	air
dish	money	child	tomato
tire	gas	soup	woman

Count Nouns		Noncount Nouns
Singular	Plural	

1   **Look at the pictures. What are the people doing? Share ideas with your classmates. Use the present continuous.**

Christmas in Mexico

The Moon Festival in China

2   **Work with a partner. Person A reads the story and answers the questions on this page. Person B reads the story and answers the questions on page 30. Then share stories with your partner.**

Christmas in Mexico
by Soraya Silas

In Mexico Christmas is a beautiful time. We have *posada*[1] from December 1 to January 6. We have parties all the time and *piñatas*[2] with candy. We have a lot of food and drinks. On December 24, the children go to bed at 8 o'clock because Santa is coming to that house. On December 31 everybody celebrates. We dance and drink. We eat *tamales*[3] or turkey, and everybody waits until 12 o'clock at night to give thanks for the New Year. I am happy to be Mexican.

1. What holiday does she tell about?

_____

2. What does her family do on this holiday?
   They have parties.
_____

_____

_____

[1]*posada*—tradition at Christmas time in Mexico when people go to different neighborhoods to perform a religious play
[2]*piñata*—a decorated container filled with candy and toys that hangs from the ceiling
[3]*tamale*—a spicy Mexican dish

Work with a partner. Person B reads the story and answers the questions on this page. Person A reads the story and answers the questions on page 29. Then share stories with your partner.

The Moon Festival
by Linda Lee

One of my favorite Chinese holidays is the Moon Festival. On this fall holiday people in China sit outside in the evening and watch the full moon. Many people eat dinner outside too. Mooncakes are a special food for this holiday. They are round, sweet pastries that look like the full moon. They're delicious!

1. What holiday does she tell about?

   _____

2. What do people in China do on this holiday? Use the simple present.
   *They eat outside.*_____

   _____

   _____

3 **What holidays do you celebrate every year? List them.**

   _____   _____

   _____   _____

   _____   _____

4 **Choose two of your holidays. Answer these questions:**

   Holiday 1   **Holiday 2**

   What is the name of the holiday?

   _____   _____

   What do you do on this holiday?

   _____   _____

   _____   _____

   _____   _____

5 **Tell a classmate about your holidays.**

6 **Write about your holidays on a separate piece of paper. Include your writing in a class booklet of holidays.**

◆ Simple Past of *Be*
  (Statements)
  (Negative Statements)
  (Yes/No Questions and Short
  Answers)
◆ *Wh*-Question: *Where*

Unit 4 Where were you?

Where was Magda at 4:30 yesterday? Tell a classmate.

Setting the Scene

Magda: Martin, it's late. Where were you?

Martin: Sorry, Mom. I was at Paul's house.

Magda: Well, I was worried. Next time, call me.

Martin: OK.

Simple Past of *Be* (Statements)

Martin was late. He was at Paul's house. He and Paul were busy.

I	**was**	late yesterday.	We	**were**	late yesterday.
He			You		
She			They		
It					

Be has two forms in the past: *was* and *were*.

1 Tell about yourself yesterday. Circle YES or NO.

1. I was tired yesterday.	YES	NO
2. I was sick yesterday.	YES	NO
3. I was in a good mood yesterday.	YES	NO
4. I was in a bad mood yesterday.	YES	NO
5. I was late to work yesterday morning.	YES	NO
6. I was at home last night.	YES	NO
7. I was at work last night.	YES	NO

2 Read your YES sentences to a classmate. Then tell the class your YES answers and give more information.

Example: A: *I was sick yesterday.*
B: *Boris and I were at home last night.*

Simple Past of *Be* (Negative Statements)

I	**wasn't**	here yesterday.
He		
She		
It		
We	**weren't**	here yesterday.
You		
They		

> Contractions:
>
> was   not
> ∨
> wasn't
>
> were   not
> ∨
> weren't

3 Look at the following pictures. Fill in the blanks with *was, wasn't, were,* or *weren't*. One person was at home last night. Who?

Julia   Paul   Octavio

1. Julia _WAS_ at the library last night. She _WASn't_ at home.

2. Paul _WASn't_ at home last night. He _WAS_ at the movies.

3. Octavio _WAS_ at home last night. He _WASn't_ at work.

4. Julia and Paul _Weren't_ at home last night. They _were_ out.

4 Write about yourself. Use *was* or *wasn't*.

1. I _WASn't_ in bed at 6:00 A.M. yesterday.

2. I _WASn't_ in bed at noon yesterday.

3. I _WASn't_ at school yesterday morning.

wasn't 4. I _WASn't_ at a friend's house yesterday afternoon.

5. I _WAS_ at home last night.

we weren't

5 Read a classmate's sentences in Exercise 4. Tell the class about the classmate.

Example: *Mei wasn't in bed at 6:00 A.M. yesterday.*

Simple Past of *Be* (Yes/No Questions and Short Answers)

Were	you we they	at home last night?	Yes,	I we they	was. were. were.	No,	I we they	wasn't. weren't. weren't.
Was	he she it	at home last night?		he she it	was.		he she it	wasn't.

6 **Find someone in the class who was *at home* last night. Get his or her signature. Then do the same for 2-7.**

> **Example:** A: Were you *at home* last night?
> B: Yes, I was. OR No, I wasn't.

Signature

1. at home _____

2. at school _____

3. at work _____

4. at a friend's house _____

5. at the grocery store _____

6. at the movies _____

7. _____ _____

Person A looks at this page only. Person B looks at page 36 only. Take turns asking questions until you get the correct answer. Write Magda's schedule yesterday.

Example: A: Was she at *the post office* at 11:30 A.M.?
B: No, she wasn't.
A: Was she at _____?

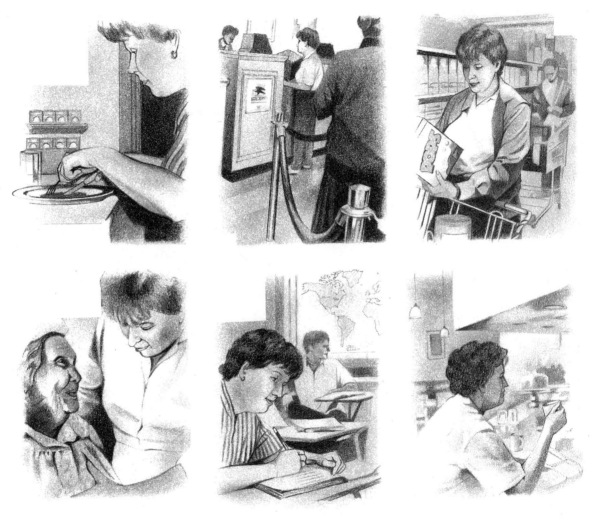

7:00 A.M.	at the nursing home
11:30 A.M.	She in the
4:00 P.M.	
4:30 P.M.	at the grocery store
6:15 P.M.	at home .
7:00 P.M.	

Person B looks at this page only. Person A looks at page 35 only. Take turns asking questions until you get the correct answer. Write Magda's schedule yesterday.

Example: B: Was she at *the grocery store* at 7:00 A.M.?
A: No, she wasn't.
B: Was she at _____?

7:00 A.M.	_____	4:30 P.M.	_____
11:30 A.M.	*at the nursing home cafeteria*	6:15 P.M.	_____
4:00 P.M.	*at the post office*	7:00 P.M.	*at her evening class*

Wh-Question: *Where*

Where	was	he	last night?	At work.
		she		
Where	were	you	last night?	At home.
		we		
		they		

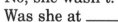

7 Find out about a classmate's schedule yesterday.

Example: A: Where were you at 6:00 A.M.?   B: *In bed.*

6:00 A.M.	_____	1:00 P.M.	_____
10:00 A.M.	_____	4:00 P.M.	_____
11:00 A.M.	_____	8:00 P.M.	_____

8 Tell the class about the classmate's schedule yesterday.

Example: *Abdul was in bed at 6:00 A.M.*

9 Listen to the conversations. Where was each person? Circle your answer.

1. Pierre   at the library   (at home)
2. Sonya   at the basketball game   (at work)
3. the man   (at the video store)   at the grocery store

Focus on Vocabulary

Community Places

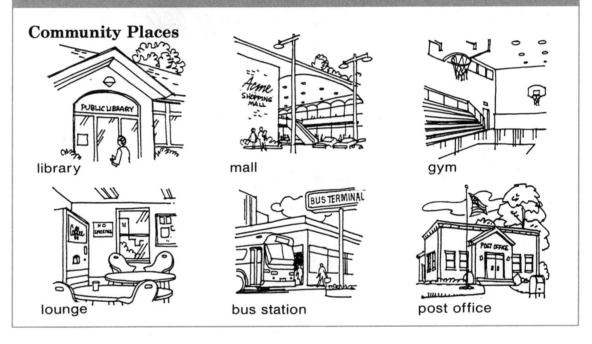

library   mall   gym

lounge   bus station   post office

10 Do you ever go to these places? Ask a classmate. Check the box.
Example: A: Do you ever go to the *library*?
          B: Yes, I *sometimes* do. OR No, I *never* do.

	often	sometimes	hardly ever	never
	Yes	*Yes*	*No*	*No*
library	Yes		No	Never
mall	Yes	Sometimes		
school gym			No	Never
school lounge			No	Never
bus station	Yes	Sometimes		
post office			No	Never

11 **Where were you Saturday afternoon? Write one place on a small piece of paper.**

Example: *the Rainbow Mall*

Your teacher will put each person's piece of paper in a bag. Choose a new paper from the bag. Who was there yesterday? Ask your classmates.

Example: A: *Abdul*, were you at *the Rainbow Mall* Saturday afternoon?
B: No, I wasn't. OR Yes, I was.

In Your Own Words

Answer these questions about yourself.

1. When is your birthday? _3/2/66_
2. Where were you on your last birthday? _I WAS AT HOME_
3. Were any people in your family with you? _YES_ Who? _MY SPOUSE AND KIDS_
4. Were you happy? _A WASEN'T HAPPY_
5. Was it a good birthday? _YES IT WAS!_

Now write about your last birthday. Use complete sentences.

On my last birthday, I

_____

_____

_____

_____

Wrapping Up

Choose a time from this list.

last night   yesterday at noon   Sunday morning
Saturday evening   this morning at 5:00   Sunday at noon

Interview six classmates. Then write their answers.

Example: A: Where were you *last night*?
B: I was *at work*.

Mario was at work last night.

Boris and Alexander were at home last night.

Victor, Ana, and Leila were at the mall last night.

♦ Simple Past
  (Statements: Regular Verbs)
  (Irregular Verbs)
  (Negative Statements)
  (Yes/No Questions and Short
  Answers)
♦ Wh-Question: *When*
♦ Wh-Question: *Why*

Unit 5 What's the message?

*Mom, have you seen my English book? Did you put it somewhere?

**Maria's children write messages and leave them on the refrigerator. They wrote
these messages yesterday.**

Setting the Scene

Maria: Did anyone call?
Tina: Yes. Anna called an hour ago, and Sylvia called about five minutes ago.
Maria: What did they want?
Tina: I don't know. Juanita talked to them. Here. She wrote these messages for you.

Mom,
Anna called at 4:00. She lost Ruth's phone number. Do you have it? Please call her tonight.
              Juanita

Mom,
Sylvia called at 5:00. She didn't leave a message.
              Juanita

Simple Past (Statements: Regular Verbs)

I	called	yesterday.	We	called	yesterday.
You			You		
He			They		
She					

Regular simple past verbs end in *-ed*.
Use the simple past to talk about an action that is completed in the past.

Look at the Appendix pages 156–157 for pronunciation rules.

1 Listen to your teacher. Is it present or past? Circle A or B.

1. (A) They talk a lot.   B: They talked a lot.
2. A: They call us.   (B) They called us.
3. A: They watch a lot of TV.   (B) They watched a lot of TV.
4. (A) They play at the park.   B: They played at the park.
5. (A) They ask a lot of questions.   B: They asked a lot of questions.

2 **Here is Maria's weekly schedule. Write about her schedule last week.**

1. Maria works every Monday. _She worked last Monday._

2. She cleans her apartment every Tuesday. _She cleaned apartmen last tuesday_

3. She calls her parents every Wednesday. _She called her parents last wednesday_

4. She walks three miles every Thursday. _She walked three miles last Thursday_

5. She bakes a cake every Friday. _She baked a cake last Friday_

6. She plays with her children every Saturday. _she played with her children last satuday_

7. She cooks a big meal every Sunday. _she cooked a big meal last Sunday_

Simple Past (Irregular Verbs)

Many verbs have a special past form. Here are some examples:

Simple Form	Simple Past	Simple Form	Simple Past
come	**came**	hear	**heard**
do	**did**	lose	**lost**
eat	**ate**	make	**made**
find	**found**	put	**put**
get	**got**	read	**read**
go	**went**	take	**took**
have	**had**	write	**wrote**

Look at the Appendix pages 158–159 for more irregular verbs.

3 **Maria's children write messages to her. Write the simple past form of the verb in parentheses.**

1. Aunt Rita called. She ___found___ your glasses. (*find*)

2. Carlos ___ate___ all the cookies, not me. (*eat*)

3. Where's my English book? I ___lost___ it. (*lose*)

4. Iris ___heard___ about a good job. Please call her. (*hear*)

5. Miguel called. He ___had___ a great time at the party. (*have*)

6. Laura called. She ___got___ a raise. (*get*)

4 Listen to these telephone conversations. Write two messages.

For _Maria_ _____ called. Message: _____ _____ _____	For _____ _____ called. Message: _____ _____ _____

5 Here are some things Maria did yesterday. Tell a classmate.

① ② ③ ④

6 This time line shows important events in Maria's life. Read the time line and complete the sentences below.

1960	1965	1970	1977	1978	1980	1983	1990
was born	**started** school	**moved** to San Juan	**finished** high school	**got** her first job	**got** married	**had** her first child	**came** to New York

1. Maria ____~~es~~ was born____ in 1960.
2. She ____started school____ in 1965.
3. She ____moved to San Juan____ in 1970.
4. She ____finished high school____ in 1977.
5. She ____got her first job____ in 1978.
6. She ____got married____ in 1980.
7. She ____had her first child____ in 1983.
8. She ____came to New York____ in 1990.

7 Make your own time line. Put five or more important events in your life on it.

8 Tell a classmate about five important events in your life. Report an important event from the classmate's time line to the class.

Example: *Cho came to the United States in 1991.*

Simple Past (Negative Statements)

I	**didn't**	have a car last year.
You		
He		
She		
We		
They		

Contraction:
did   not
↓
didn't

Use *didn't* in speaking and informal writing.

9 These pictures show Maria in 1980 and 1990. How was her life different? Tell the class.

1980—Puerto Rico

1990—New York

Example: In 1980 Maria didn't have any children.

In 1990 she had three children.

10 How was your life different ten years ago? Write three sentences. Tell a classmate.

_____

_____

_____

Simple Past (Yes/No Questions and Short Answers)

Did	you he she it we they	work yesterday?	Yes,	I he she it we they	**did.**	No,	I he she it we they	**didn't.**

11 Ask a classmate about yesterday. Check YES or NO for each question. Add two more questions.

A: Did you *have a good day* yesterday?
B: Yes, I did. OR No, I didn't.

	YES	NO
have a good day read the newspaper listen to the radio talk to friends eat a good meal hear a funny story _____ _____	✓	

12 Report your partner's YES answers to the class.

Example: *François had a good day yesterday.*

Wh-Question: *When*

When did	I you she he we they	come to the United States?	In 1990.

13 **When did you come to the United States? Ask your classmates. Line up by date of arrival. Then tell about your classmates.**

Example: *Mei came to the United States in 1993.*

Partnerwork   ▶ Person A

These famous people came to the United States from other places. Do you know who they are? Person A looks at this chart only. Person B looks at the chart on page 46 only. Ask your partner the questions below and fill in your chart.

When did _____ come to the United States?
What did _____ do in the United States?

Name	When did they come to the U.S.?	What did they do?
Females		
Martina Navratilova	1975	_____
Gloria Estefan	_____	became a singer
Males		
An Wang	1945	_____
Roberto Clemente	_____	played baseball
Alexander Graham Bell	1871	_____

These famous people came to the United States from other places. Do you know who they are? Person B looks at this chart only. Person A looks at the chart on page 45 only. Ask your partner the questions below and fill in your chart.

When did _____ *come to the United States?*
What did _____ *do in the United States?*

Name	When did they come to the U.S.?	What did they do?
Females		
Martina Navratilova	_____	became the world's top female tennis player
Gloria Estefan	1959	_____
Males		
An Wang	_____	started a computer company
Roberto Clemente	1955	_____
Alexander Graham Bell	_____	invented the telephone

14 Here are some important events in U.S. history. When did they happen? Can you guess the year?

1783   **1850**   **1861**   **1876**   **1969**

1. The first person landed on the moon in _____.
2. The United States became an independent country in _____.
3. Alexander Graham Bell invented the telephone in _____.
4. California became a state in _____.
5. The American Civil War started in _____.

15 Write a sentence about an important event in the history of your native country. Tell your classmates about it.

_____

_____

Past Time Expressions

Write today's date: _____
(month, day, year)

Write the correct year in the parentheses below.

My sister and her husband went to Alaska **last year**. (_____)
They went to Alaska **a year ago**. (_____)
They had their first child **the year before last**. (_____)
They had their first child **two years ago**. (_____)
They moved to Portland **three years ago**. (_____)
They got married **five years ago**. (_____)

Write the month in the parentheses.

My brother and his wife had a baby **last month**. (_____)
They had a baby **a month ago**. (_____)
They bought a car **six months ago**. (_____)

Write the date in the parentheses.

I am working hard **today**. (_____)
I took a trip **yesterday**. (_____)
My friend left the day before **yesterday**. (_____)
He left **two days ago**. (_____)

 16 **Fill in the chart. Use past time expressions from the box above. Add two more questions and the names of three classmates.**

When did you . . . ?				
1. come to the U.S.				
2. get married				
3. get your first job				
4. start school				
5. take a vacation				
6. see a good movie				
7.				
8.				

Wh-Question: Why

Why did | I you she he we they | come to the United States?   I came here because. . . .

Why did you come to the United States?

Why asks for a reason.

Use *because* to give a reason or explanation.

17 **Match the questions and answers. Write the letter(s) after the question. More than one answer is possible.**

1. Why did you go to the grocery store?   a. Because I was tired.

2. Why did you take the bus?   b. Because I don't have a car.

3. Why did you leave early?   c. Because I needed some bread.

4. Why did you walk home?   d. Because I fell in love.

5. Why did you get married?   e. Because my feet hurt.

6. Why did you _____?   f. Because _____

Wrapping Up

What did you do last weekend? Write three sentences. Write each sentence on a small piece of paper. Put your pieces of paper in a bag. Then choose three other pieces of paper. Find the people who wrote those sentences.

Example: A: Did you *see a good movie*?
             B: Yes, I did. OR No, I didn't.

♦ *There is/There are*
(Statements)
(Questions and Short
Answers)
♦ Commands
♦ Verb + Preposition + Object

Unit 6   Is there a post office nearby?

Nam and Hanh live on Franklin Street. Where do you live?

Setting the Scene

José: Excuse me. Is there a post office nearby?

Hanh: Yes, there is. Go straight ahead three blocks and turn right. It's the second building on the right.

José: Thanks.

Hanh: You're welcome.

There is/There are (Statements)

Singular	Plural
There is a Laundromat.	**There are** some trees.
There's a shoe repair shop too.	**There are** many buildings too.
There isn't a post office.	**There aren't** any banks.

Use the contractions in speaking and informal writing.

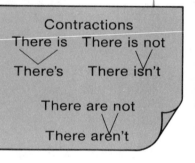

Contractions

There is → There's

There is not → There isn't

There are not → There aren't

1 **What's on Franklin Street? Study the picture on page 49. Make two lists. Use *there's* or *there are*.**

Singular	Plural
_____	_____
_____	_____
_____	_____
_____	_____
_____	_____

2 **Think about your street or neighborhood. Do you like it? Write your reasons. Use *there's*, *there isn't*, *there are*, and *there aren't*.**

I like my neighborhood because *there are many stores nearby.*

_____

_____

There is/There are (Questions and Short Answers)

There is a grocery store on Main Street.

Is there a grocery store on your street?	**Yes, there is.** **No, there isn't.**
Are there any stores on your street?	**Yes, there are.** **No, there aren't.**

---

3 **What's near your school? Answer these questions. Circle YES or NO. Then compare answers with your classmates.**

1. Is there a bank nearby? YES NO

2. Is there a movie theater nearby? YES NO

3. Is there a public library nearby? YES NO

4. Is there a zoo nearby? YES NO

5. Is there a Laundromat nearby? YES NO

4 **Ask about a classmate's neighborhood or workplace. Check YES or NO. Tell the class what you found out.**

A: Is there a *post office* in your neighborhood?

B: Yes, there is. OR No, there isn't.

A: Are there any *restaurants* in your neighborhood?

B: Yes, there are. OR No, there aren't.

	YES	NO
post office	✓	
restaurants		
museum		
bank		
school		
stores		
trees		
park		
hospital		

Prepositions of Place

Is there a restaurant nearby?
Yes, there is. It's **on the southwest corner of** Main Street and Front Street.

Is there a shoe store nearby?
Yes, there is.　　It's **across from** the post office.
　　　　　　　　It's **next to** the restaurant.
　　　　　　　　It's **between** the restaurant and the bookstore.

5　Use the map on this page. Read these sentences. Circle TRUE or FALSE.

1. There's a post office on Main Street.　　　　　　TRUE　FALSE

2. There's a deli across from the bank.　　　　　　TRUE　FALSE

3. There's a drugstore between the bank and the　　TRUE　FALSE
jewelry store.

4. There's a bakery on the southeast corner of Main　TRUE　FALSE
Street and Front Street.

5. There's a jewelry store next to the drugstore.　　TRUE　FALSE

6　Use the same map on this page. Answer the questions with *across from*, *on the corner of*, *next to*, or *between*.

1. Is there a drugstore on Front Street?
　　Yes, there is. It's across from the jewelry store.

2. Is there a restaurant on Main Street?
　　_____

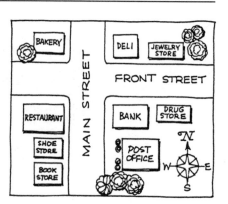

3. Is there a shoe store on Main Street?
　　_____

4. Is there a movie theater on Front Street?
　　_____

5. Is there a bakery on Main Street?
　　_____

6. Is there a deli on Front Street?
　　_____

Ordinal Numbers

Rita lives on the **first** floor.

1st	first
2nd	second
3rd	third
4th	fourth
5th	fifth
6th	sixth
7th	seventh
8th	eighth
9th	ninth
10th	tenth

Ordinal numbers tell the order or position of things.

7 What floor do they live on? Write the answers. Compare your answers with a classmate.

1. Rita lives on the first floor.
2. _____
3. _____
4. _____
5. _____
6. _____
7. _____
8. _____
9. _____
10. _____

8 This is a building directory. Complete the sentences below. Tell about the offices in the building.

> **Hancock Building**
> 234 Emory Street
>
> | | Suite |
> |---|---|
> | Capri Beauty School | 318 |
> | Carlyle Jewelers | 209 |
> | Landry & Landry Law Office | 612 |
> | Lennox Copy Shop | 211 |
> | Mahoney Construction Company | 421 |
> | New Horizons Travel Agency | 514 |
> | Simpson Car Rental Company | 102 |
> | Stephanie's Flower Shop | 105 |

1. There's a _____ on the third floor.

2. There's a flower shop on the _____ floor.

3. There's a jewelry store on the _____.

4. There's a _____ on the fifth floor.

5. There's a law office on the _____.

6. _____.

7. _____.

8. _____.

9 Look at the map. Where are these buildings? Write the location. Use ordinal numbers and *on the left* or *on the right*.

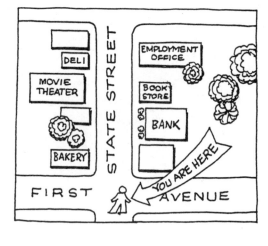

1. Where's the bakery?
   It's the first building on the left.

2. Where's the bank?
   _____

3. Where's the bookstore?
   _____

4. Where's the movie theater?
   _____

5. Where's the deli?
   _____

6. Where's the employment office?
   _____

Commands

Use commands to give directions.

A: Excuse me. How do I get to the shoe store?
B: **Go straight ahead. Cross** Elm Street. It's the first building on the right.

A: Excuse me. How do I get to the bank?
B: **Turn left** at the next corner. It's the second building on the right.

A: Excuse me. How do I get to the post office?
B: **Walk** to Elm Street and **take a right**. It's the second building on the left.

10   Look at the map. Finish these conversations. Write the questions.

1. A: Excuse me. How do I get to
    _____?

   B: Walk to Elm Street and turn left. It's the second building on the right.

2. A: _____?
   B: Turn right at the next corner. It's the first building on the right.

3. A: _____?
   B: Go straight ahead. Cross Elm Street. It's the second building on the right.

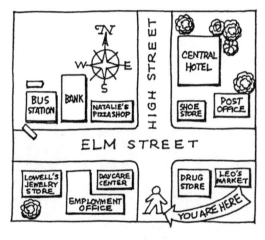

Small Talk

Work with a partner. Practice this conversation. Use the map on this page.

A: How do I get to *Lowell's Jewelry Store?*
B: *Take a left on Elm Street. It's the third building on the left.*

1. the bus station
2. Leo's Market
3. the shoe store
4. the post office
5. Natalie's Pizza Shop

Activities

What are these people doing? Match the people on the left with the phrase on the right. Then make a complete sentence about each person.

1. Mei is _____
2. Fred is _____
3. Clara and Eva are _____
4. Sylvia and Karen are _____
5. José is _____

a. **waiting for** the bus
b. **asking for** directions
c. **looking at** a sign
d. **talking to** a friend
e. **listening to** the radio

Ramón   François   Thuy   Rita   Magda

11 **What are these people doing? Tell a classmate. Use one of these verbs.**

wait for   listen to   look at

ask for   talk to

Example: *Rita is looking at a dress.*

Verb + Preposition + Object

Hanh is looking at **Mrs. Patel**.
Hanh is looking at **her**.

François is talking to **Pierre**.
François is talking to **him**.

Ramón is looking for **his book**.
He is looking for **it**.

Maria is waiting for **Tina and Juanita**.
Maria is waiting for **them**.

Magda is waiting for **you and me**.
Magda is waiting for **us**.

Object Pronouns	
me	us
you	you
him	them
her	
it	

12 Practice this conversation with a partner.

A: Did you *talk to Ramón* yesterday?
B: Yes, I did. I *talked to him* in the morning.

1. talk to Maria
2. talk to Tina and Juanita
3. look for my book
4. listen to the news program

5. wait for Mr. Park
6. look for your keys
7. wait for Ms. Bustami
8. talk to Mr. Davis

Partnerwork   ▶ Person A

Person A looks at this map only. Person B looks at the map on page 58 only. Ask questions and listen to your partner's directions. Label the building on the map. Then listen to your partner's question and give directions. Ask for:

1. coffee shop
2. bookstore
3. supermarket
4. bank

A: Is there a *coffee shop* nearby?
B: Sure. There's a *coffee shop on First Street*.
A: How do I get there?
B: *Walk to First Street and turn left. It's the second building on the left.*
A: Thanks.

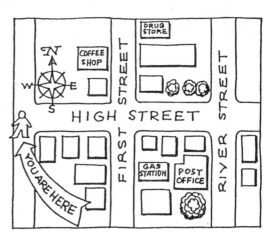

Person B looks at this map only. Person A looks at the map on page 57 only. Ask questions and listen to your partner's directions. Label the building on the map. Then listen to your partner's question and give directions. Ask for:

1. coffee shop ✓
2. drugstore
3. gas station
4. post office

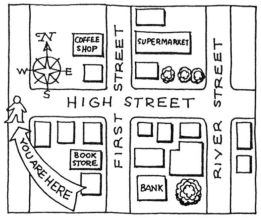

A: Is there a *coffee shop* nearby?
B: Sure. There's a *coffee shop on First Street.*
A: How do I get there?
B: *Walk to First Street and turn left. It's the second building on the left.*
A: Thanks.

In Your Own Words

Think of a favorite place. Where is it? Why do you like it? Tell a classmate about it.

Wrapping Up

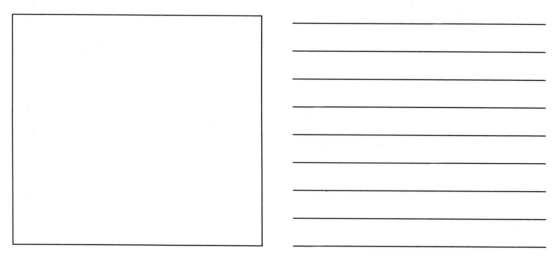

Draw a map of your neighborhood. Name the streets. What places do you go to in your neighborhood? Show them on your map. Then choose one place. Tell how to get there from your home. Write the directions.

Map	Directions
	_____
	_____
	_____
	_____
	_____
	_____
	_____
	_____
	_____
	_____

Review: Units 4–6

1 **December 22, 1990, was an important day for James St. Fleur.
Look at the picture. What do you think happened?**

2 **Here is Mr. St. Fleur's story.**

An Important Event in My Life
by James St. Fleur

One of the important events in my life was on December 22, 1990,
when my second son was born. I didn't have the chance to watch when
my older children were born. In Haiti, they don't allow the father to be
in the delivery room.

My wife started labor very early in the morning, and I couldn't wait to
see my son born. I drove my wife to the hospital. They put her in a room.
The nurses and doctors checked on her several times. Finally, they asked
me to put on a hospital gown, and they took her to the delivery room. In
less than an hour the baby came. The doctor gave me a pair of scissors
and asked me to cut the baby's umbilical cord. I was very excited to see
how my baby came into the world.

3 Tell about Mr. St. Fleur's important event. Write complete sentences.

1. What happened on December 22, 1990?

_____

2. How did his wife get to the hospital?

_____

3. What did he wear in the delivery room?

_____

4. How did he help with the birth of his son?

_____

5. How did he feel when his son was born?

_____

6. How old is his son now?

_____

4 On another piece of paper, make a time line. Tell what happened in the story. Then use your time line to retell the story.

Example:

```
_____|_____|_____
```
He drove his wife to   He cut the umbilical
the hospital.   cord.

5 Choose an important event in your life. Tell about it on a time line. Think about these questions as you write:

Where were you?
What happened first?
What happened next?
How did you feel?

6 Tell a classmate about the important event in your life. Listen to your classmate's story. Then tell your classmate's story to another pair of students.

7 Write about the important event in your life. Include your story in a class booklet.

♦ Comparative Adjectives with *-er*
♦ Choice Questions and Answers with *One*
♦ Comparative Adjectives with *More*
♦ Possessive Adjectives and Pronouns

Unit 7 Which one is cheaper?

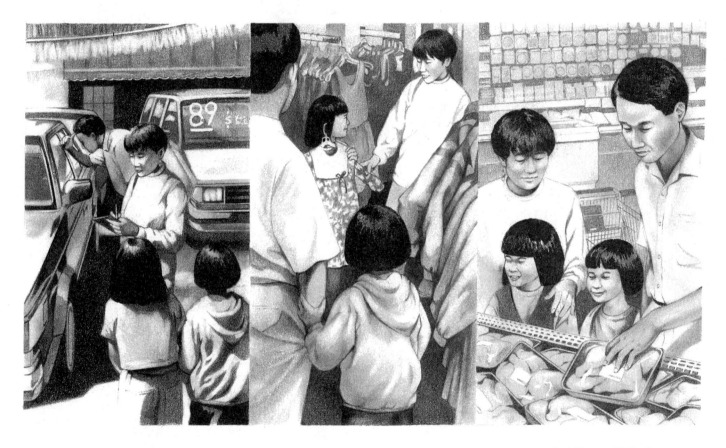

Hanh and Nam went shopping for a car, for clothing, and for food. How did they decide what to buy?

Setting the Scene

Hanh likes the van because it's bigger.

Nam bought chicken because it's cheaper than pork.

Chau likes the blue dress because it's prettier.

Comparative Adjectives with -er

The van is **bigger than** the sedan.
Chicken is **cheaper than** pork.
The blue dress is **prettier than** the white dress.

van   sedan

Adjectives	→ Comparatives	Adjectives	→ Comparatives
large	larger	fast	faster
big	bigger	slow	slower
small	smaller	cheap	cheaper
old	older	pretty	prettier
new	newer	ugly	uglier
good	better	bad	worse
far	farther		

Look at the Appendix on page 160 for spelling rules.

1 Which car do you like? Why? Tell a classmate.

Example: *I like the van. It's newer.*
I like the van because it's newer.

the van or the station wagon

the sports car or the sedan   the sedan or the station wagon

2 These advertisements are from a newspaper. Which car do you like better? Why?

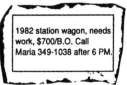

> 1982 station wagon, needs work, $700/B.O. Call Maria 349-1038 after 6 PM.

> 1986 sedan, 4 door, new tires, spotless, $2150. Days 549-5849

3 Work with a partner. Compare these items by price. Make sentences like the example.

Example: *A vacuum cleaner is cheaper than a 20-inch color TV.*

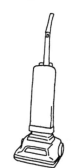
upright vacuum

2 slice toaster

boy's bike

electric box fan

slimline phone

color TV

AM/FM stereo radio with cassette

1. A vacuum cleaner is cheaper than a color TV.
2. A boy's bike is bigger than slice Toaster.
3. A boy's bike is faster than a
4. A
5. A
6. A
7.

4 Which is cheaper? Circle your answer. Compare answers with your classmates. Then check your answers at the supermarket.

1. (a pound of chicken) OR a pound of beef
2. a quart of milk OR (a quart of juice)
3. a pound of butter OR (a pound of margarine)
4. a pound of grapes OR (a pound of oranges)
5. (a pound of spinach) OR a pound of carrots
6. a pound of rice OR (a pound of spaghetti)

Choice Questions and Answers with *One*

Which car is cheaper, the old car or the new car?

old car  new car

The old car. (The old car is cheaper than the new car.)

Which car is cheaper?	**Which** car is bigger?
The old car.	The new car.
The old **one**.	The new **one**.
(The old car is cheaper than the new one.)	(The new car is bigger than the old one.)

Use *one* in place of the noun.

---

5 **Look at the small car and the large car. Answer the questions. Use *one* in your answer.**

1. Which car is cheaper? _The large one_____
2. Which car is faster? _____
3. Which car is safer? _____
4. Which car is newer? _____

6 **Choose two cars from the picture. Write three questions with *which*. Read your questions to a partner. Your partner will answer them.**

Example: *Which car is faster, the van or the sportscar?*

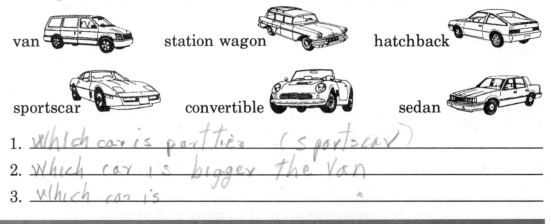

van   station wagon   hatchback

sportscar   convertible   sedan

1. _which car is prettier (sportscar)_
2. _Which car is bigger the van_
3. _which car is_

Comparative Adjectives with *More*

Pork is *more expensive* than chicken.

The big suitcase is *more useful* than the small one.
The blue dress is *more attractive* than the green one.

Adjectives	**Comparatives**
expensive	more expensive
useful	more useful
attractive	more attractive

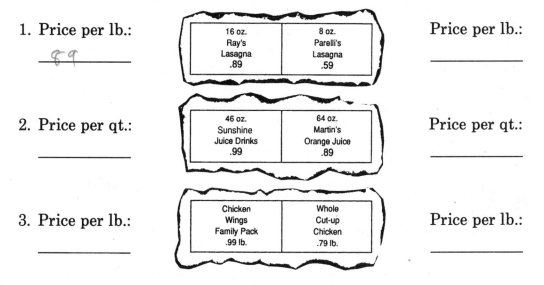

pork   chicken

Look at the Appendix on page 160 for when to use *more*.

7 Which is more expensive? Read the amounts carefully. Compare answers with a classmate. Use the Appendix on page 160.

1. Price per lb.:

   _89_

   | 16 oz. Ray's Lasagna .89 | 8 oz. Parelli's Lasagna .59 |

   Price per lb.:

   _____

2. Price per qt.:

   _____

   | 46 oz. Sunshine Juice Drinks .99 | 64 oz. Martin's Orange Juice .89 |

   Price per qt.:

   _____

3. Price per lb.:

   _____

   | Chicken Wings Family Pack .99 lb. | Whole Cut-up Chicken .79 lb. |

   Price per lb.:

   _____

8 Which of these household appliances is more useful to you? Why? Compare ideas with a partner.

Example: Which appliance is more useful, *a coffee maker or a rice cooker?*

coffee maker or rice cooker   wok or frying pan   mixer or blender

Focus on Vocabulary

Describing People

Carl is heavier than Mark.
Mark is taller than Carl.

*Use heavier. Don't use fatter.
It's more polite.*

Adjective	→	Comparative
tall		taller
short		shorter
fat		fatter
heavy		heavier
thin		thinner
old		older
young		younger
pretty		prettier
handsome		more handsome

Adjective	→	Comparative
shy		shyer
friendly		friendlier
nice		nicer
smart		smarter
funny		funnier
happy		happier
polite		more polite
helpful		more helpful
athletic		more athletic
artistic		more artistic

Look at the Appendix on page 160 for spelling rules.

9 **Work with a partner. Answer the questions below. Write two sentences.**

Example: Say: *Trang is taller than I am.* OR *Trang is taller than me.*
Write: *Trang is taller than I am.*

1. Who is taller?

_____

2. Who is more active?

_____

10 **Who is more talkative than you? Who is more artistic? Interview four people in your class. Then write one or two sentences.**

Example: *Raul, May, and Pantha are more talkative than I am. Sonya is more artistic than I am.*

1. _____

2. _____

Possessive Adjectives and Pronouns

Miguel's hair is longer than **my hair**.
Miguel's hair is longer than **mine**.

Tanya's hair is curlier than **your hair**.
Tanya's hair is curlier than **yours**.

Ron's hair is shorter than **his hair**.
Ron's hair is shorter than **his**.

Ron

my hair	→ mine
your hair	→ yours
his hair	→ his
her hair	→ hers
our hair	→ ours
their hair	→ theirs

11 Work with a partner. Answer these questions about you and your partner. Write *mine*, *his*, or *hers*. Brenda and Maria

1. Whose hair is longer? My hair is longer.
2. Whose hair is curlier? Her hair isn't curlier.
3. Whose hands are bigger? Her hands are bigger.
4. Whose fingernails are shorter? Her fingernails are shorter.

12 Write four sentences about you and your partner. Use the information from Exercise 11. Then tell another pair of students about you and your partner.

Example: *My hair is longer than hers.*
Her fingernails are shorter than mine.

My hair is longer than hers. ✓

Her fingernails aren't shorter than mine. •

My hair isn't curlier ~~with that~~ than hers. ✓

Her hands are bigger than mine. ✓

13 Listen to the sentences. Look at the picture of Ron. Who am I? Circle me.

Ron   1   2   3   4   5   6

Use What You Know

Write the comparative form of these adjectives. Then use each word in a sentence to compare two things or two people.

1. sweet _sweeter_   2. heavy _heavier_   3. small _smaller_
4. beautiful _more beautiful_ 5. big _bigger_   6. thin _thinner_
7. cold _colder_   8. tall _taller_   9. useful _more useful_

1. _Ice cream is sweeter than milk._
2. _The van is heavier than sedan car._
3. _My pencil is smaller than hers._
4. _The new sedan is more beautiful than old sport car._
5. _This dog is bigger than his._
6. _Brenda is thinner than mine._
7. _Dicember is colder that July._
8. _Maricela is taller than Carmen._
9. _The big box is more useful than the small box._

In Your Own Words

Think of someone in your family. How are you different? Write your ideas. Use comparative adjectives.

Example: *My sister Barbara is older than I am.*
She is shyer than I am.
She is more artistic than I am.
I am happier than she is.

1. _____
2. _____
3. _____
4. _____

Wrapping Up

Work with your classmates. Line up according to height. Taller people stand behind you. Shorter people stand in front of you. Follow the model in the picture.

♦ Future with *going to*
(Statements)
(Yes/No Questions and Short
Answers)
♦ *Wh*-Questions with *going to*
♦ *Wh*-Question: *How*
♦ *Need to, Want to, Plan to*

Unit 8 What are you going to do?

Children's Day is a popular Vietnamese holiday. Children often march in a parade on this holiday. When is your country's next holiday? What are your plans for that holiday?

Setting the Scene

Hanh: Tomorrow is Vietnamese Children's Day, and there's going to be a parade downtown. Can you and Martin come?

Magda: Sure. We'd love to. Are Chau and Thuy going to be in the parade?

Hanh: Yes, they are. But I'm not going to be in the parade, so we can watch together.

Future with *going to* (Statements)

I	**am**	(I'm)	**going to** watch the parade tomorrow.
He	**is**	(He's)	
Hanh	**is**	(Hanh's)	
She	**is**	(She's)	
You	**are**	(You're)	
We	**are**	(We're)	
They	**are**	(They're)	

> We always write *going to*, but we often say "gonna."
> *I'm "gonna" watch the parade tomorrow.*

1 **What are you going to do tomorrow? Write three activities.**

1. _I'm going to visit friends tomorrow._

2. _____

3. _____

4. _____

2 **Read a partner's sentences. Tell the class about your classmate. Put your classmate's answers into two groups.**

Recreation	Chores
Example: *Juan is going to go to a party tomorrow.*	*He is going to do the laundry.* *He's going to clean his room.*

Yes/No Questions and Short Answers

Are	you	going to visit friends?	Yes,	I am.	No,	I'm not.
Are	we			we are.		we're not.
Are	they			they are.		they're not.
Is	she			she is.		she's not.
Is	he			he is.		he's not.

3 What are your classmates going to do on Saturday? Choose one of these activities or use your own. Ask all of your classmates. Count the number of Yes answers and report the number to the class. Together answer the questions below.

Example: A: Are you going to *go shopping* on Saturday?
  B: *Yes, I am.* OR *No, I'm not.*

Activity	Number of Yes Answers
go shopping	✓✓✓ – 3
visit friends	
go to the movies	
clean the house	
take a trip	
play soccer	
go dancing	
watch TV	

1. Which activity are *many* of your classmates going to do?

   Many of my classmates are _____

2. Which activity is *no one* going to do?

   No one is _____

4 Where's Martin going to go after school? What's he going to do in each place? Tell a partner your ideas.

Wh-Questions with *going to*

What	are	we	going to	bring?
What		you		wear?
When		you		go?
Where		they		go?
What	is	he		do?
When		she		go?
What		it		do?

Wh-questions start with a question word. The rest of the word order is like a yes/no question.

5 **Read this invitation and answer the questions.**

You're invited to:

WHAT: a birthday party for Maria Sánchez

WHEN: on August 23, at 7 PM

WHERE: 23 Hanover Street, Apt. 3

RSVP 555-1819

1. When's the party? _____

2. Who's it for? _____

3. What kind of party is it? _____

4. Where is the party going to be? _____

5. What are you going to wear? _____

6. What are you going to do there? _____

6 **What about you? Work with a partner. Ask each other questions with *what*, *when*, and *where*. Follow the example.**

1. I'm going to go to the party *at 7:00.* _When are you going to go to the party?_

2. I'm going to wear *black pants and a blue sweater.* _____
   _____

3. I'm going to bring *some flowers.* _____

4. I'm going to talk *with friends there.* _____

5. I'm going to go home *at 11 P.M.* _____

7 Invite your classmates to a party. Fill in this invitation. Exchange invitations with a partner. Tell about your partner's party.

> *You're invited to:*
> WHAT: _____
> WHEN: _____
> WHERE: _____
>
> RSVP _____

Example: *Mei is going to have a party at the Szechuan Taste restaurant. She is going to have the party on March 22 at noon. They are going to celebrate her husband's birthday.*

_____

_____

_____

_____

8 What holiday are you going to celebrate next? Write the name of the holiday on a piece of paper. Exchange papers with a partner. On another piece of paper, write several questions about your partner's holiday. Exchange papers again and answer your partner's questions.

Example: Name of holiday: *Vietnamese New Year's Day*

What are you going to do on New Year's Day?   *I'm going to watch the Dragon Dance.*

Where are you going to be on New Year's Day?   *I'm going to be at home.*

When are you going to celebrate New Year's Day?   *Next month.*

Who are you going to be with on New Year's Day?   *My family.*

Wh-Question: *How*

How are you going to get home from class?	by car
	by bus
	by subway
	by train
	on foot

Use *how* to ask about the means of transportation.

Small Talk

Practice this conversation with a partner.

A: Where are you going?
B: To *the mall*.
A: How are you going to get there?
B: *By bus*.

 9   Ask a partner. Where are you going to go after class? How are you going to get there?

Need to, Want to, Plan to

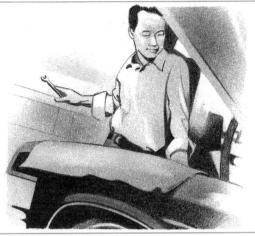

need to + verb
> I **need to** talk to you.
> Nam **needs to** buy a new car.

want to + verb
> I **want to** take a trip.
> Hanh **wants to** learn Spanish.

plan to + verb
> I **plan to** get a new job.
> François **plans to** take the train.

10 **Think of three things you need to do. Think of three things you want to do. Write them on the lines below.**

need to do	want to do
1. *I need to go to the supermarket.*	1. *I want to visit my sister.*
2. _____	2. _____
3. _____	3. _____
4. _____	4. _____

11 **Exchange your *need to do* and *want to do* lists with a partner. Tell the class about your partner.**

Example: *Noy needs to go to the supermarket.*

12 **Look at the movie section in your newspaper. Then practice this conversation. Invite a classmate to go to the movies. Then tell the class about your plans.**

A: Do you want to go to the movies tonight?

B: Sure. What movie do you want to see?

A: How about *Gone With the Wind*?

B: Sounds good. When do you want to go?

A: How about 7?

B: OK. See you then.

"Frankly, my dear..."

Example: *We are going to see* Gone With the Wind *tonight at 7.*

What are you going to do next weekend? List things that you need to do (*I need to* . . .). List things that you want to do (*I want to* . . .). Then make your plan (*I plan to* . . .).

Things I need to do	Things I want to do
_____	_____
_____	_____
_____	_____
_____	_____

Things I plan to do

_____

_____

_____

_____

_____

Wrapping Up

Look again at the dialogue on page 70. Tell what each of these people is going to do at the parade.

1. Hanh *is going to watch the parade.*
2. Magda _____
3. Thuy _____
4. Chau _____
5. Martin _____

What do you think they are going to do after the parade? Write your ideas.

_____

_____

_____

◆ Superlative Adjectives
  with *-est*
  with *most*
◆ *Wh*-Question: *Which*
◆ *Whose/Who's*
◆ Gerunds with *like* and *hate*

Unit 9   Who's the youngest?

This is Thuy's family. Who is older than Thuy?

Setting the Scene

Laurie: I hate being the youngest person in my family!

Thuy: Why is that, Laurie?

Laurie: Because I never get new clothes. I always get my older sister's clothes.

Thuy: I like being the youngest person in the family.

Laurie: Really! Why?

Thuy: Because there's always someone to help me with my homework.

Superlative Adjectives with -est

Thuy is the **youngest** person in her family.

Adjective	→ Superlative	Adjective	→ Superlative
tall	the tallest	short	the shortest
big	the biggest	small	the smallest
old	the oldest	young	the youngest
fast	the fastest	slow	the slowest
pretty	the prettiest	ugly	the ugliest
good	the best	bad	the worst
far	the farthest		

Look at the Appendix on page 161 for spelling rules.

1 Write the superlative form of these adjectives. Then use the words to tell about the people in your family or other people you know.

Adjective	→ Superlative	Adjective	→ Superlative
1. shy	*the shyest*	4. quiet	_____
2. funny	_____	5. young	_____
3. tall	_____	6. old	_____

Example: *My brother's the shyest person in my family.*

2 **Work with a group of students. Answer these questions. Write the person's name on the line.**

1. Who's the quietest person in your group? _____

2. Who's the funniest person? _____

3. Who's the busiest person? _____

4. Who's the luckiest person? _____

3 **Work with a partner from your community. Answer these questions. If possible, locate each place on a map of your area.**

1. Where's the best supermarket? _____

2. What's the busiest street? _____

3. Where's the largest park? _____

4. What's the tallest building? _____

5. What's the best restaurant? _____

4 **Work with a group of students. Answer these questions. Compare answers with another group. Look at the maps on pages 168–171. Then check the answers on page 176.**

1. What's the largest country in South America? _____

2. What's the smallest country in South America? _____

3. What's the largest country in Asia? _____

4. What's the smallest country in Europe? (shown on the map) _____

5. What's the largest state in the United States? _____

6. What's the smallest state in the United States? _____

7. What state is the farthest south in the United States? _____

Superlative Adjectives with *Most*

My couch is the **most** expensive piece of furniture in my home.

Adjective → Superlative

Adjective	Superlative
expensive	the most expensive
useful	the most useful
dangerous	the most dangerous
important	the most important
popular	the most popular

Look at the Appendix on page 161 for when to use *the most*.

5 What's your opinion? Write your ideas. Then compare ideas with a classmate.

1. What is the most expensive vegetable?

   _____

2. What is the most expensive car?

   _____

3. What is the most expensive way to travel?

   _____

4. What is the most useful kitchen appliance in your home?

   _____

5. What is the most dangerous sport?

   _____

6. What is the most beautiful place in your native country?

   _____

6 Work with a partner. Put these items in order by cost. Write the most expensive item first. Write the cheapest item last.

1. _____   2. _____   3. _____   4. _____

hair dryer   camera   lamp   flashlight

Wh-Question: *Which*

Which chair is the most comfortable?   The one on the left.
Which chair is the cheapest?   The one on the right.
Which chair is the oldest?   The one in the middle.

 7   **Work with a partner. Take turns asking and answering questions. Use the words below or your own words.**

1. tall   old   tired   athletic   short

Example: *Which woman is the most tired?*
The one on the right.

2. long   fancy   pretty   expensive   cheap

Example: *Which dress is the most expensive?*
The one on the left.

3. comfortable   old   fancy   expensive   nice   cheap

Example: *Which pair of shoes is the most comfortable?*
The one in the middle.

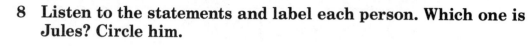

8 **Listen to the statements and label each person. Which one is Jules? Circle him.**

_____ _____ _____ _____ _____ _____ _____

Work with a partner. Take turns asking and answering questions about the people.

Example: _Which one is Jean?_
Jean is the tallest one.

Whose/Who's

Whose grandmother is in the picture?
   Thuy's.

Who's in the picture?
   Thuy and her grandmother.

The pronunciation of _Whose_ and _Who's_ is the same. The meanings are very different. _Whose_ asks about possession. _Who's_ means _Who is_.

9 **Listen and write the questions. Use _whose_ or _who's_ correctly. Then ask a classmate.**

1. _Who's the tallest person in the class?_
2. _____
3. _____
4. _____
5. _____
6. _____

Gerunds with *like* and *hate*

Laurie **hates being** the youngest person in her family.
She doesn't **like wearing** her sister's old clothes.

I **like**	**dancing**. **driving**. **going** to the beach.	He **hates**	**getting** up early. **doing** the laundry. **cooking**.

Use the verb + *-ing* after *like* and *hate*.
(You can also say *I like to dance, He hates to get up early.*)

10 What chores around home do you hate doing? Write them on the lines below. Compare lists with your classmates. Which household job is the most unpopular?

1. *I hate washing the floor.* _____

2. _____

3. _____

4. _____

11 Get together with three classmates. Think about your childhood. Find three things that you all hated doing and three things that you all liked doing. Tell the class.

Example: A: I hated *washing* dishes. Did you?
B: Yes, I did. OR No, I didn't.

hated doing

1. _____

2. _____

3. _____

liked doing

1. _____

2. _____

3. _____

12 What do you like doing in class? With the teacher, write your ideas on this brainstorming diagram.

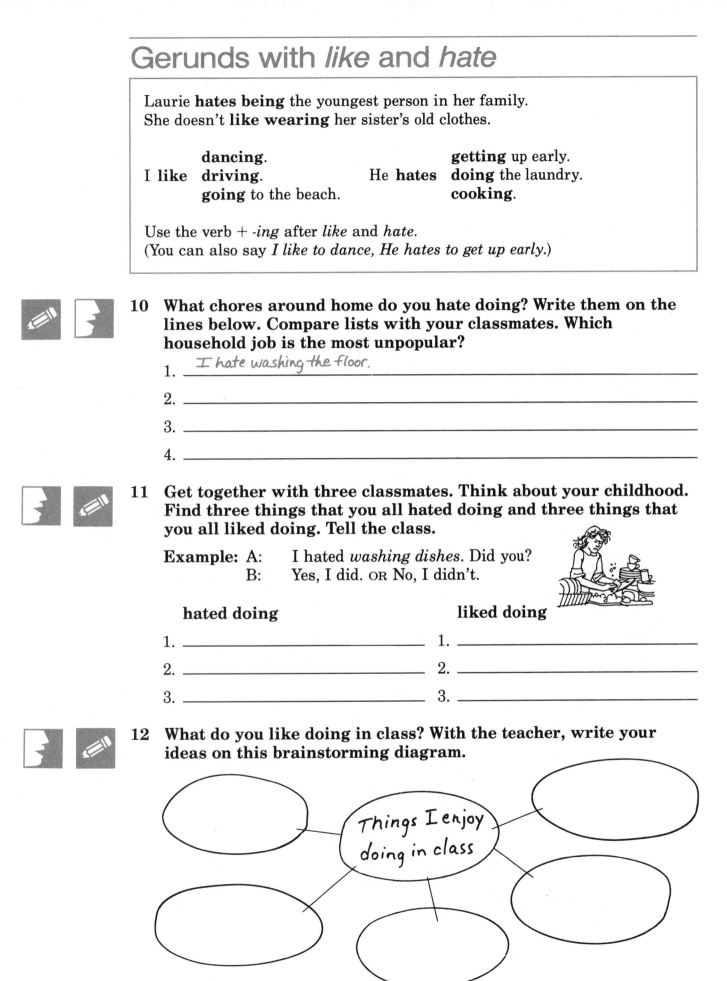

Things I enjoy doing in class

In Your Own Words

What was your best day or worst day last week? Think about what happened on this day. Write your ideas on a brainstorming diagram like this one.

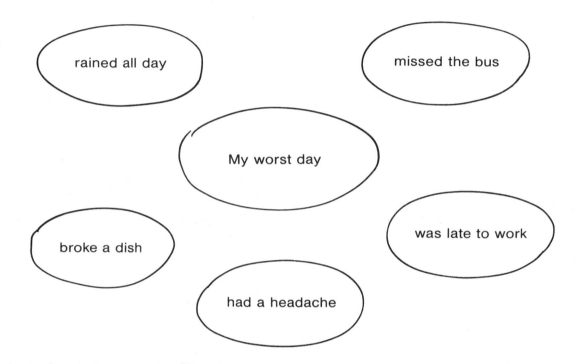

rained all day

missed the bus

My worst day

broke a dish

was late to work

had a headache

Now write a paragraph about what happened on that day. Use your brainstorming diagram for ideas.

Wrapping Up

These pairs of adjectives are opposites. Write the superlative of each adjective. Then use the words to tell about yourself, your family, or your friends.

1. young *the youngest*

2. tall _____

3. shy _____

4. quiet _____

5. funny _____

6. old _____

7. short _____

8. outgoing _____

9. talkative _____

10. serious _____

I am the youngest person in my family.

_____

_____

_____

_____

Use the map of the United States on page 168 to answer these questions. Use complete sentences.

1. What places in the United States do you want to visit?

   _____

2. Which state do you live in now?

   _____

   Is Connecticut bigger or smaller than your state?

   _____

   Is Montana bigger or smaller than your state?

   _____

3. Look at the western part of the United States. Which state is the smallest—Washington, Oregon, or California?

   _____

4. Look at the northeastern part of the United States. Which state is the largest—Maine, New Hampshire, or Vermont?

   _____

5. Put these states in order from the largest to the smallest: Florida, Maryland, Rhode Island, South Carolina, Texas.

   largest _____

   _____

   _____

   _____

   smallest _____

6. The Great Lakes are between Canada and the United States. How many lakes are there? _____

Put the lakes in order from the largest to the smallest.

largest _____

_____

_____

_____

smallest _____

7. Next week Anita is going to drive from Florida to New York. Which states is she going to travel through?

_____

_____

_____

8. Plan a trip from your state to another state far away. Then answer these questions.

Which state are you going to visit?

_____

Which states are you going to travel through?

_____

_____

Tell the class about your plans.

9. Tell about a town or city that you know well. Compare it to the town or city in which you live now. Write your ideas on another piece of paper. Then tell your classmates about the place.

Example: Beibei, China

> *Beibei is a beautiful city. It's smaller than Los Angeles, but it's more crowded. In the summertime, it's very hot in Beibei. It's hotter than in Los Angeles.*

Unit 10 Can you go?

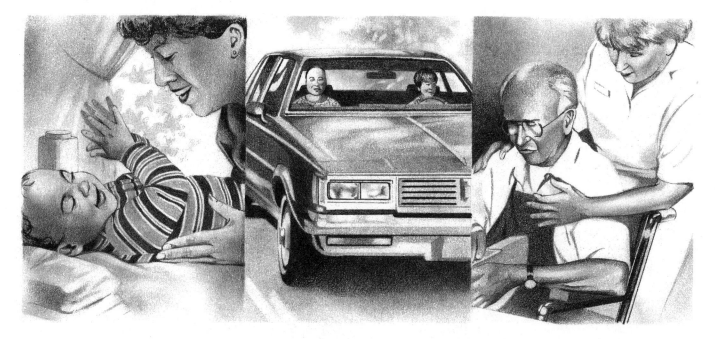

Rita wants to go to the movies. Who do you think can go with her? Who can't go with her? Why not?

Setting the Scene

Rita wants to go to the movies tonight, but her friends can't go.

Maria can't go because she has to take care of Pablo.

Hanh can't go— she has to take her mother-in-law to ESL class.

Magda can't go because she has to work.

She is going to ask her brother because he doesn't have to work tonight.

Have to (Statements)

I	**have to**	work tomorrow.	Juan	**has to**	work tomorrow.
You			He		
We			Magda		
They			She		

Use *have to* to talk about something that is necessary.

> We always write *have to* and *has to*.
> We often say "hafta" and "hasta."

1 What do you have to do tomorrow? Make a list.

1. *I have to cook dinner.* 4. _____
2. _____ 5. _____
3. _____ 6. _____

Have to (Questions and Short Answers)

Do	I	**have to** work tomorrow?	Yes,	you	do.	No,	you	don't.
	you			I			I	
	we			we			we	
	they			they			they	
Does	she			she	does.		she	doesn't.
	he			he			he	

2 **Look at each activity on your list. Find someone in the class who has to do the same thing. Then tell the class about yourself and your classmate. Follow the model below.**

A: *Irene*, do you have to cook dinner tomorrow?
B: No, I don't.
A: *José*, do you have to cook dinner tomorrow?
C: Yes, I do.

Report to the class:
A: *José* and I have to cook dinner tomorrow.

3 **Fill in your schedule for next Saturday and Sunday. List the things you have to do.**

	Saturday	**Sunday**
Morning	fix my car	
Afternoon		
Evening		

4 **Now tell the class what you have to do on Saturday and Sunday. Make complete sentences with *have to*.**

Example: *On Saturday I have to fix my car.*

5 **Use your schedule from Exercise 3. Invite different classmates to do something next weekend. Fill in the chart with their answers.**

Example: A: *Do you want to go out for coffee on Saturday morning, Ali?*
B: *I'm sorry. I can't. I have to fix my car.*

Name	**Can**	**Can't**	**Why not?**
Ali			He has to fix his car.

Don't have to (Negative Statements)

I You We Ramón and Maria They	**don't**	**have to**	get up early tomorrow. It's a holiday.
He Rita She	**doesn't**		*Don't have to* means *it's not necessary.*

6 **How is Sunday different from the rest of the week? Write your ideas. Use *don't have to* in your sentences.**

Example: *On Sunday, my kids don't have to go to school.*
On Sunday, my wife doesn't have to go to work.

_____

_____

_____

_____

7 **Listen to these conversations. Check YES or NO. Who has to go to work tomorrow?**

	YES	NO
Ramón		
François		
Nam		
Hanh		

Can and *Can't* of Opportunity

I	**can**	go to the party.	I	**can't**	go to the movies.
You			You		
Paul			He		
He			Maria		
She			She		
We			We		
They			They		

Contraction:
cannot
∨
can't

I can means *I have the opportunity* to do something. *I can't* means *I don't have the opportunity*. We usually say *can't*. We sometimes say *cannot* when we want to emphasize something we can't do.

8 **Look at the picture on page 88. Rita wants to go to the movies. Who can go with her? Write *can* or *can't*.**

1. Maria _____ go. She has to take care of Pablo.

2. Hanh _____ go. She has to take her mother-in-law to her ESL class.

3. Magda _____ go. She has to work.

4. Rita's brother _____ go. He doesn't have to work tonight.

Very + Adjective

Anna didn't sleep much last night. She is **very** tired today.

Boris has a bad cough, a sore throat, and a fever of 103°F. He is **very** sick.

The word *very* makes an idea stronger.

9 **Complete these sentences with *very* + adjective.**

funny   excited   busy   sad   tired   sleepy

1. Paul has to do a lot of things today. He's _____.

2. His little sister is crying. She's _____.

3. Miguel stayed up late last night. He's _____ today.

4. Susan likes to tell jokes. She's _____.

5. I _____. I'm _____.

Can and Can't of Ability

I	**can** play	the guitar.	I	**can't**	lift 500 pounds.
You			You		
He			He		
She			She		
We			We		
They			They		

I can means *I am able to.*   *I can't* means *I am not able to.*

10 **Listen to your teacher. Do you hear *can* or *can't*? Circle A or B. Then practice with a partner.**

1. A: I can swim.   B: I can't swim.

2. A: She can speak Spanish.   B: She can't speak Spanish.

3. A: He can play the guitar.   B: He can't play the guitar.

4. A: We can dance.   B: We can't dance.

5. A: They can type fast.   B: They can't type fast.

6. A: I can lift 100 pounds.   B: I can't lift 100 pounds.

11 **What do you know about these people? Think of things each of these people can or can't do. Tell your classmates.**

Example: *Maria can speak Spanish.*
She can't speak Russian.

1. Maria   2. Ramón   3. Hanh   4. Nam   5. Magda   6. Martin

Personal Skills

Check (✓) the things you can do.

Home and Workplace Skills

> draw
> sew
> cook
> type/keyboard
> drive a car
> drive a truck
> read a map
> use an electric saw

Social Skills

> tell stories
> make people laugh
> make small talk
> speak a second language
> dance

Sports

play	Ping-Pong
	soccer
	football
	baseball
	basketball
	volleyball
	tennis

> swim
> bowl
> box

12   What can these people do? Write your ideas.

Example: *A bilingual person can speak two languages.*

1. An artist _____

2. A TV comedian _____

3. A taxi driver _____

4. A tailor or seamstress _____

Can (Questions and Short Answers)

| Can | you
he
she
we
they | dance? | Yes, | I
he
she
we
they | can. | No, | I
he
she
we
they | can't. |

13 Find someone in the class who can *dance*. Get his or her signature. Add two questions of your own.

A: Can you *dance*?
B: Yes, I can. OR No, I can't.

1. dance _____

2. play the piano _____

3. type _____

4. braid hair _____

5. tie a necktie _____

6. play tennis _____

7. sing _____

8. sew _____

9. swim _____

10. speak three languages _____

11. _____ _____

12. _____ _____

14 Think of three things you can do. Think of three things you can't do but want to learn to do. Make two lists.

Can Do	Can't Do
I can sew.	*I can't swim*

15 Look at your *Can't Do* list from Exercise 14. Find a classmate who can do each thing. Then write about it.

Example: A: *Cara*, can you *swim*?
     B: No, I can't.
     A: *Antonio*, can you *swim*?
     C: Yes, I can.

I can't swim, but Antonio can.
_____

16 Which sports do you have to play indoors? Which ones do you have to play outdoors? Which sports can you play indoors or outdoors? Put them into three groups. (Answers may vary.)

soccer   baseball   basketball
volleyball   swimming   bowling (American)
football   boxing   Ping-Pong

Indoor Sports	Outdoor Sports	Indoor or Outdoor Sports
_____	_____	_____
_____	_____	_____
_____	_____	_____
_____	_____	_____

17 Work in a group. Write the languages each person can speak.

Example:

Name	Ngoc	Antonio	Boris
Languages	Vietnamese French English	Spanish English	Russian English

18 Work with your classmates. List the languages spoken in your class. Count the number of speakers of each language. On a piece of paper, write about your class.

Example:

Language	Number of Speakers
English	14
Spanish	8
Vietnamese	3
Russian	2
Tagalog	2
French	1

In my class, fourteen people can speak English. Also, eight people can speak Spanish, three people can speak Vietnamese, two people can speak Russian, two people can speak Tagalog, and one person can speak French.

Think about where you live now. Think about where you lived before. What can you do now? What can't you do now? Write your ideas.

_____

_____

_____

_____

_____

Wrapping Up

Think of things Pablo and Juanita can't do. Think of things they have to do. Write your ideas. Then compare with a partner.

Pablo (eight months old)

He can't go to school. He has to stay at home.

_____

_____

_____

_____

Juanita (ten years old)

She can't drive to school. She has to take the bus.

_____

_____

_____

_____

Unit 11   I'll do it later

Maria is angry. Can you guess why? What does she want to do?

Setting the Scene

Maria: Carlos and David, it's time to do your homework.

David: We'll do it later, Mrs. Sánchez. We promise.

Maria: You'll be very sleepy later.

Carlos: No, we won't. We really want to watch this show. We'll turn the TV off in ten minutes.

Maria: OK. But don't forget. You'll do your homework in ten minutes.

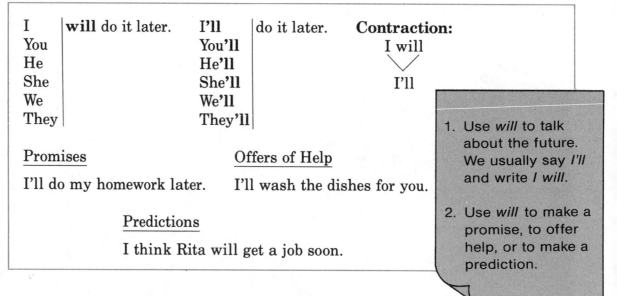

Future with *Will*

I	**will** do it later.	**I'll**	do it later.	**Contraction:**
You		**You'll**		I will
He		**He'll**		
She		**She'll**		I'll
We		**We'll**		
They		**They'll**		

Promises

I'll do my homework later.

Offers of Help

I'll wash the dishes for you.

Predictions

I think Rita will get a job soon.

1. Use *will* to talk about the future. We usually say *I'll* and write *I will*.

2. Use *will* to make a promise, to offer help, or to make a prediction.

1 Listen to your teacher. Is the sentence present or future? Circle A or B. Then practice with a partner.

1. A: I walk fast.   B: I'll walk fast.

2. A: He drinks coffee.   B: He'll drink coffee.

3. A: She drives to work.   B: She'll drive to work.

4. A: We do our best.   B: We'll do our best.

5. A: You work hard.   B: You'll work hard.

6. A: They ride the bus to school.   B: They'll ride the bus to school.

2 Work with two or three classmates. Plan one page of a class newsletter. Each person will offer to do something. Write the person's name and job on the blank lines.

Example: _____Laura_____   _Write a news story about the class._

1. _____ _____
2. _____ _____
3. _____ _____
4. _____ _____

Tell the class about your plan.

Example: *Laura will write a news story about the class.*

Write your news stories.

3 Think of four things you need to do. Write what you need to do and when you will do it.

What do you need to do?	When will you do it?
pay the electric bill	on Friday

Tell the class when you will do each thing.

Example: *I'll pay the electric bill on Friday.*

4 What do you think Maria will do? Write your predictions.

1. Pablo is in his playpen. He is crying.
   She will pick him up.

2. Maria is feeding Pablo. The telephone rings.

   _____

3. Carlos doesn't want to go to school because he has a headache.

   _____

Meanings of *Won't*

I **will not** be late.	I **won't** be late.	Contraction:
You	You	will not
He	Ramón	↘
She	Tina	won't
It	It	
We	We	
They	They	

Promises
I **won't** lose your book.

Refusals
We **won't** eat this food. It's horrible!

Predictions
Paul **won't** get that job.

> Use *won't* to make a promise, a refusal, or a prediction.

5 **Maria's children always make promises. Can you guess what they say? Write your ideas. Use *won't* in your sentences.**

1. Tina wants to go shopping with a friend. What promise does she make to her mother?

   I won't be late.

2. Juanita wants to wear her mother's scarf. What promise does she make? _____

3. Carlos wants to ride his bike outside. What promise does he make?

   _____

4. Tina wants to use her mother's camera. What promise does she make?

   _____

6 **Practice this conversation with a partner. Then make new conversations with the information in 1-5.**

A: Martin won't get up.
B: Why not?

A: Because he's tired.

1. get up/is tired
2. do the dishes/hates doing the dishes
3. get off the phone/wants to talk to his friend
4. turn down the radio/likes loud music
5. clean up his room/is busy
6. _____ / _____

Wh-Questions with Will

Questions	Predictions
Nam's car isn't working. **How** will he get to work?	He'll get to work **by bus**.
Hanh bought a new couch. **Where** will she put it?	She'll put it **in the living room**.
Maria wants to have a party. **Who** will she invite?	She'll invite **her friends**.
Ramón wants to drive from Chicago to Los Angeles. **How long** will it take?	It'll take **two or three days**.

7 **Work with a partner. How long will it take Ramón to do these things? Compare answers with another pair of students.**

1. shave ___It will take 10 minutes to shave.___
2. get a haircut _____
3. read the newspaper _____
4. wash the car _____
5. buy groceries for a week _____

_____ Total Time

8 **Read these statements. Write a question with *will* for your partner. Your partner will write an answer to your question. Read your partner's prediction.**

Example: Ramón forgot to take his lunch to work.

Question: *What will he eat for lunch?*
Prediction: *He'll buy a bowl of soup, a sandwich, and a cup of coffee.*

1. Maria wants to visit her mother in Puerto Rico.

Question: _____

Prediction: _____

2. Ramón hopes to buy a new car.

Question: _____

Prediction: _____

Review of Questions

Rita is planning a trip to Ecuador. Here are some questions to ask her.

Are you planning a trip?	What are you planning?
Are you going to go to Ecuador?	Where are you going to go?
Are you going to go soon?	When are you going to go?
Can you speak Spanish?	What language can you speak?
Will Laura be there?	Where will Laura be?
Do you have to get a visa?	What do you have to get?
Will you go by plane?	How will you get there?
Will it take long to get there?	How long will it take to get there?
Did you go there last year?	When did you go there?

These questions ask about the present, past, or future.

9 **Listen to the question. Is it present, past, or future? Circle the correct answer.**

1. Present   Past   Future

2. Present   Past   Future

3. Present   Past   Future

4. Present   Past   Future

5. Present   Past   Future

10 **Read the questions below. Listen to the conversation between Maria and Rita. Write the answers in sentences.**

1. What is Rita doing now? _____

2. Did she call Laura? _____

3. When will she call her? _____

11 **Read the answers below. Listen for the questions in the conversation between Rita and Laura. Then write the questions.**

1. _____
   To the passport office.

2. _____
   Yes, I did.

3. _____
   Yes. I'll be there at six o'clock.

Future Time Expressions   Date _____

Write the **year** in the parentheses.

Maria will probably visit her brother **next year**. (_____)

Ramón plans to visit Puerto Rico **in a year**. (_____)

I plan to go back to school **the year after next**. (_____)

François will probably get a new job **in a few years**. (_____)

Write the **month** in the parentheses.

Rita will be in Ecuador **next month**. (_____)

Maria plans to take a vacation **in two months**. (_____)

My vacation starts **six months from now**. (_____)

Write the **day** in the parentheses.

I'll do it **tomorrow**. (_____)

I'm going to leave **the day after tomorrow**. (_____)

I plan to leave **in three days**. (_____)

---

12 **Tell about your plans for the future. Use some of these time expressions in your sentences.**

next week	next month	next year
the week after next	the month after next	the year after next
in a few weeks	in a few months	in a few years

1. _I plan to take a trip next year._____

2. _____

3. _____

4. _____

5. _____

6. _____

This joke is from Bulgaria. Read it aloud with a partner. Then write your own version of the joke on another piece of paper. Share it with the class.

A father said to his sons:

"Tomorrow your mother is going to bake a pie. Who is going to eat it?"

The oldest son replied:

"Father, I'll eat it all!"

The father then said:

"Tomorrow I am going to butcher a pig. Who is going to eat it?"

The same son answered:

"Father, I'll eat it all!"

The father added:

"Tomorrow we are going to plow the field. Who is going to plow?"

The oldest son answered again:

"It's always me, always me. Now it's somebody else's turn to volunteer."

Wrapping Up

You just won the lottery! The jackpot totaled $2,000,000! What are you going to do with all that money? Write your ideas.

_____

_____

_____

_____

- *Might*
- *Too* + adjective
- *Not* + adjective + *enough*
- *Very, Too, Enough*
- Suggestions with *Let's*

Unit 12 It might be a book

Hanh received a package in the mail. What do you think is in her package? When was the last time you received a package? What was it? Who was it from?

Setting the Scene

Thuy: Mom, we got a package in the mail!

Hanh: Who's it from?

Thuy: Uncle Thang. What do you think it is?

Hanh: I don't know, Thuy. It might be a book.

Thuy: No, it can't be. It's too light.

Hanh: Really? Well, then, it might be some food.

Laurie: I don't think so. It's too small. Do you think it's a game?

Hanh: I don't know. Let's open it and find out.

Might

It **might** be a pair of earrings.
It **might** be a watch.
It **might** be a ring.

I	
He	
She	**might** go to the party.
We	
You	
They	

Use *might* when you are not sure about something.

1 Work with a partner. What might be in these packages? Write your ideas below. Compare your ideas with two other students.

1. _____

2. _____

3. _____

4. _____

5. _____

6. _____

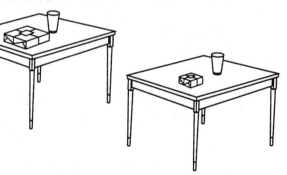

2 **Where might these people be? Read the clues and list several possibilities. Write sentences with *might*. Share your ideas.**

1. It's seven o'clock at night, and Hanh is sitting in a dark room. She is wearing pants and a sweater. Where might she be?

   _____

   _____

   _____

2. Martin is taking a shower, but he's not at home. Where might he be?

   _____

   _____

   _____

3. Nam is eating Vietnamese noodles, but he's not at home. Where might he be?

   _____

   _____

   _____

3 **A "droodle" is a special kind of picture. Identifying droodles is a kind of game. What do you think the droodles below are? Think of several possibilities. Compare ideas with your classmates.**

Example: *It might be a spoon. It might also be a bottle.*

1.

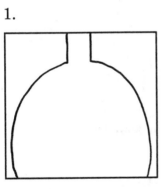

2.

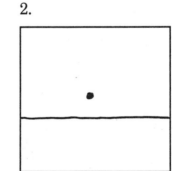

3.

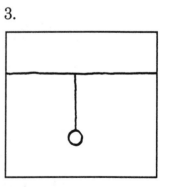

4 **Listen to your teacher. After each conversation, complete a sentence. Use *might* or *will*.**

1. She _____ go to Rita's house.

2. She _____ do the dishes later.

3. He _____ eat lunch at Sam's house.

4. He _____ pick up his friend at 7:00.

Opposites

Which adjectives from each list describe the pictures?

Clothing

large	small
long, tall	short
heavy	light
thick	thin
strong	weak

Food

cooked	raw
sweet	sour
bland	spicy
mild	hot
fresh	stale
fresh	spoiled
ripe	unripe

Furniture

loose	tight
comfortable	uncomfortable
neat	messy
hard	soft
sharp	dull

Equipment

useful	useless
difficult	easy
expensive	cheap
sick	well

Too + adjective

Mel can't do these things. Why not?

He can't touch the ceiling. He's **too short**.

He can't go to work. He's **too sick.**
He can't play basketball. He's **too tired**.

Too + adjective means there is a problem. We cannot do the activity when we are too sick, or too tired, or too busy, etc.

5 Why can't these people go out today? Write a sentence with *too*.

Tina   Maria   Ramón

6 Work with a partner. Follow the model. Add your own question.

A: Can you *drink a cup of lemon juice*?
B: No, I can't. It's too *sour*. Can you? OR Yes, I can. Can you?
A: Yes, I can. OR No, I can't.

1. eat a quart of ice cream
2. eat a hot pepper
3. drink a glass of grapefruit juice
4. drink a cup of espresso coffee
5. _____

7 Write *very* or *too*.

1. Espresso coffee is _____ strong. I can't drink it.

2. This tea is _____ good. It's just right!

3. Martin is _____ tired, but he is going to go to school.

4. Ramón is _____ sick. He can't go to work.

Not + Adjective + Enough

Simon can't do these things. Why not?

He can't wear his brother's clothes because he's
not big enough. (He's **too small.**)
He can't open the door because he's **not tall enough.**
(He's **too short.**)
He can't go to school because he's **not old enough.**
(He's **too young.**)

Not enough means not all that is necessary to do something.

8 **Rewrite these sentences. Use *not* + adjective + *enough*.**

Example: Simon can't touch the ceiling because he's too short.

Simon can't touch the ceiling because he's not tall enough.

1. Fred can't get a driver's license because he's too young.
2. Mr. Johnson can't get out of bed because he's too weak.
3. Pablo can't play in the pool because the water's too cold.
4. Laura can't cut the meat because the knife is too dull.

9 **Complete these conversations. Use *not* + adjective + *enough*. Then practice with a partner.**

1. What's the matter?
   I can't cut this paper. The scissors are _____.

2. What's wrong?
   I can't sit in this chair. It's _____.

3. Are you going to wear your blue shirt?
   No, I'm not. It's _____.

4. Are you going to go swimming?
   I don't think so. The water is _____.

5. Did you buy Ray's old car?
   No, I didn't. It wasn't _____.

Very, Too, Enough

This banana is **very** ripe. It's yellow and a little soft. I'll eat it for lunch.
That banana is **too** ripe. It's black and mushy. I can't eat it. Throw it away!
That banana is **not** ripe **enough**. It's green and hard. I can't eat it today,
but I might eat it the day after tomorrow.

10 Write *very*, *too*, or *enough*.

1. This banana is _____ ripe. I won't eat it.

2. This coffee is _____ strong. I like it that way.

3. The coffee is not sweet _____. I can't drink it without more sugar.

4. This tea is _____ weak. It tastes like water. I won't drink it.

5. This cake is _____ good. It's perfect! Can I have another piece?

Suggestions with *Let's*

Let's go to the movies tonight.
Let's call Rita.
Let's have spaghetti for dinner tonight.

Use *let's* to make a suggestion that includes you and the person(s) you are talking to.

Let's = Let us   We almost always say and write *Let's*.

Small Talk

Work with a partner. Practice this conversation.

A: *It's raining.* What do you want to do?
B: Let's *go to the movies.*
A: I don't want to *go to the movies. I saw a movie yesterday.* Let's *play cards.*
B: Okay.

1. It's snowing.
2. There's no food in the house.
3. I have $100.
4. _____

In Your Own Words

What are your future plans? List your ideas. Share your ideas with a partner.

Things I will definitely do: Things I might do:

(I am sure.)   (I'm not sure.)

_____   _____

_____   _____

_____   _____

_____   _____

_____   _____

Wrapping Up

Arrange your chairs in a circle. One person makes a request. Each classmate gives a different excuse, speaking in order around the circle. Continue until someone can't think of an excuse. That person gets a point. (The person with the fewest points at the end wins.)

Example:
(Request)   A: Irma, can you *drive me to the airport*?
(Excuse)   B: Sorry, I can't. *I have to work.* OR *I'm too tired.* OR *My car isn't working*.

Requests:

Can you clean the board for me?
Can you sweep the classroom floor?
Could you please lend me your car for the weekend?
Could you please _____?

1 **Read the signs on the door below and answer the questions. Write complete sentences.**

```
┌─────────────────────────────────────┐
│                                     │
│           Store Hours               │
│          Mon-Sat  10-9              │
│            Sun  12-8                │
│                                     │
│  No Food, Beverages, or Smoking Please │
│            No Bare feet             │
│       MasterCard/Visa Accepted      │
│                                     │
└─────────────────────────────────────┘
```

1. What do people have to wear in this store?

   _____

2. When does the store open on Tuesday?

   _____

3. Can you shop in this store on Sunday morning?

   _____

4. When does the store close on Friday?

   _____

5. What can't you do in this store?

   _____

6. Can you pay for your purchases with a credit card?

   _____

2 **Person A looks at this page only. Person B looks at page 114 only. Ask questions to complete sign B. Then answer your partner's questions about sign A.**

Sign A   Sign B

```
┌─────────────────────────────┐    ┌─────────────────────────────┐
│                             │    │                             │
│   Beijing Restaurant        │    │  Bruno's Grocery Store      │
│        OPEN                 │    │         Hours               │
│  Mon & Tue 11:30 A.M. - 10 P.M. │    │ Mon - Thur _____ - 7 P.M. │
│ Wed, Thur, & Sun 11:30 A.M. - 1 A.M. │    │   Fri - Sat 7 A.M. - _____  │
│  Fri & Sat 11:30 A.M. - 2 A.M.  │    │     Sunday _____        │
│                             │    │       No _____          │
└─────────────────────────────┘    └─────────────────────────────┘
```

Person B looks at this page only. Person A looks at page 113 only. Answer your partner's questions about sign B. Then ask questions to complete sign A.

Sign A   Sign B

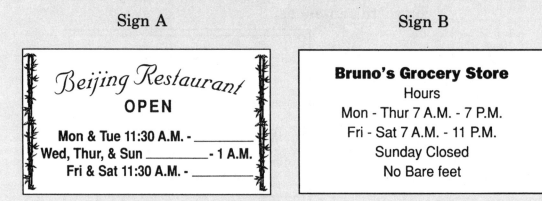

3   **Read these names and guess the type of business.**

Example: *The Children's Castle might be a children's clothing store.* OR *It might be a day-care center.*

1. The Children's Castle   5. The Growing Tree

2. Beautiful Music   6. The Happy Traveler

3. Yum Yum Shop   7. The Lovely Lady

4. The Write Store   8. The Picture Shop

4   **Work with a partner. What do these signs mean? Write your ideas.**

Sign	What does it mean?
Quarters Only	*You have to use quarters.*
Shirt Required	_____
No Parking	_____
Emergency Exit	_____

5   **Read the sentences below and answer the questions.**

1. Don is going to use the emergency exit to leave the building. What will happen when he opens the door?

_____

2. Tanya parked in a no-parking area. What might happen?

_____

3. Alicia is going to a restaurant, but she isn't wearing shoes. What might the server say to her?

_____

Unit 13 Please turn it down

Magda wants Martin to do something. What do you think it is?

Setting the Scene

Magda: Martin, turn down the radio. I'm on the phone.
Martin: What? I can't hear you.
Magda: The radio is too loud. Please turn it down.
Martin: Sure. (*Martin turns the radio down a little.*) Is that OK?
Magda: A little more, please.
Martin: OK. (*He turns it down a little more.*) How's that?
Magda: That's better. Thanks.

Review of Commands

There are different ways to tell or ask a person to do something. The way we tell or ask often depends on the situation.

Emergency:
Be careful!

Watch out!

Urgency:
Hurry up!

Instructions:
Cook the rice for 30 minutes.
Don't overcook it.

1 What might you say in these situations? Write a command.

1. An old man is starting to cross the street and a car is coming.

_____

2. You and your friend are at a coffee shop. You both have class in ten minutes. You already finished your coffee, but your friend is still drinking his. You are going to be late for class.

_____

3. You are walking with a friend. You see a hole in the sidewalk ahead.

_____

4. You are walking on a sidewalk. A person on a bicycle comes quickly toward you. You think he is going to run into you.

_____

5. Your roommate asks you how to make a sandwich.

_____

Commands and Requests

Commands	Polite Commands
Affirmative	

Turn down the radio.	Please turn down the radio.
Be home by 8 o'clock.	Please be quiet.
Open your books to page 110.	Please open your books to page 110.
Listen to this conversation.	Please do Activity 2.

Negative

Don't slam the door.	Please don't talk.
Don't be late for lunch.	Please don't be late.

Requests

Affirmative

Help me.	Could you please help me?
Come in.	Would you please come in?

Negative

Don't smoke.	Would you please not smoke?

Please makes a command more polite. Tone of voice can also make a command more polite.

Requests are the most polite way to ask a person to do something. Tone of voice can make a request sound rude.

2 **What do you think Magda says to Martin? Write an affirmative command and a negative command for each situation.**

1. Martin left his jacket and shoes on the floor in the living room.

   Please put away your things.

   Don't leave your jacket in the living room.

2. Martin is making a lot of noise.

   _____

   _____

3. It is almost time for dinner. Martin is looking for something to eat in the kitchen.

   _____

   _____

4. It's 11 P.M. and Martin is watching TV.

   _____

   _____

3 **Magda is at work at the nursing home. What might she say? Can she say it another way? Which do you think is the best way?**

1. Magda's patient needs to sleep and some noisy visitors are coming in. They are laughing loudly.

   Be quiet. OR *Please be quiet.* OR *Would you please be quiet?*

2. A visitor arrives. He is smoking a cigarette. What should Magda say?

   _____

3. A visitor is in a patient's room. He is going to open a window, but the patient is cold.

   _____

4. Magda needs help lifting her patient out of bed. An aide is nearby.

   _____

5. Magda is carrying three boxes of supplies. Her arms are full. She can't open the door.

   _____

Responses to Commands and Requests

Affirmative Responses	Negative Responses
A: Wait a minute!	A: Please show me your driver's license.
B: **Sure.** OR **OK.**	B: **I'm sorry. I can't. I don't have one.**
A: Would you please read this?	A: Would you please read this?
B: **I'd be glad to.** OR **Of course.**	B: **I'm really busy now. Could I read it later?**

4 Match the commands and requests on the left with the responses on the right.

—— 1. Wait a minute!

—— 2. Could you please close the window?

—— 3. Don't smoke in here.

—— 4. Please be quiet.

—— 5. Could you please help me?

—— 6. Would you please read this?

a. Of course.

b. Sure.

c. OK.

d. I'm sorry.

e. I'm really busy now. Could I read it later?

f. I'd be glad to.

5 Respond to these commands and requests. Practice with a partner.

1. A: Please hurry up!

   B: _____

2. A: Would you please close the door?

   B: _____

3. A: Please show me your I.D.

   B: _____

4. A: Could you please help me with this?

   B: _____

Two-Word Verbs

Martin **turned down** the radio because his mother was on the telephone.
Peter **turned on** the TV because he wanted to watch the soccer game.
Mei **turned off** the heat because the room was too hot.
Laura **turned up** the radio because she couldn't hear the music.

Two-Word Verbs	Meaning
turn up	make the volume louder
turn down	make the volume softer
turn on	start a machine
turn off	stop a machine

Some verbs have two words. The two words together usually have a different meaning from the meanings of the separate words.

6 Finish the conversations. Use two-word verbs. Then practice with a classmate.

1. A: It's too noisy.

   B: _Oh, I'll turn down the radio._

2. A: I can't hear the TV show.

   B: _____

3. A: I would love to listen to some music.

   B: _____

4. A: No one's watching the TV show.

   B: _____

7 Match the solution on the right with the problem on the left.

____ 1. Hanh was cold.   a. He turned off the light.

____ 2. It was too dark to read.   b. Martin turned it down.

____ 3. Carlos wanted to sleep.   c. Maria turned on the light.

____ 4. The iron was too hot.   d. She turned up the heat.

Common Two-Word Verbs

Use the words and ideas around these two-word verbs to guess their meaning.

Laura **called up** her friend. They talked for one hour.
Maria **called off** her party because she was sick.
Peter **gave up** smoking a week ago. He already feels much better.
François **cleaned up** his apartment before his guests arrived.
He **put away** all his clothes.
He **picked up** his parents at the airport.
How did you **find out** Laura's age? Did she tell you?
Boris borrowed Ana's camera and radio last week. He **gave back** the camera today.

Look at Appendix pages 162–163 for a list of two-word verbs.

8 **Work with a classmate. Fill in the blanks with a two-word verb from the list. Then practice the conversation.**

call up	clean up	give up	call back
find out	call off	give back	

Two roommates are talking about a neighborhood baseball game.
They are getting ready for a party after the game.

A: Would you please _____ the living room? It's a mess! Some friends are coming over after the baseball game.
B: Oh, when will the game start?
A: I'm not sure. Let's _____ the coach and _____. (*calling him up*) Oh. His line is busy. We'll have to _____ later.
B: Well, they might _____ the game because it's starting to rain now.
A: I hope they don't. Do we have enough snacks for the party?
B: I think so. But don't serve any potato chips. Irene is trying to _____ junk food because she wants to lose weight.
A: Don't worry. I won't. Don't forget to _____ the CDs we borrowed after the party.
B: I won't.

Separable Two-Word Verbs

Magda: Martin, please **turn down** the radio.
Martin: What? I can't hear you.
Magda: I said, "Please **turn** the radio **down**."
Martin: OK, I'll turn it down.

You can separate many two-word verbs with a noun or an object pronoun. Here are some separable two-word verbs:

turn . . . up	call . . . off	find . . . out
turn . . . down	call . . . up	put . . . on
turn . . . on	clean . . . up	put . . . away
turn . . . off	pick . . . up	give . . . back
call . . . back	write . . . down	look . . . up

A noun can go after or between the two parts.
A pronoun can go only between the two parts.

Object Pronouns:

me	us
you	you
him	them
her	
it	

9 Complete these requests with two-word verbs and object pronouns. Then practice with a partner.

1. A: I need to look up a word. Would you please __*give back*__ my dictionary?

   B: OK. I'll give __*it*__ back in a minute.

2. A: Smoking is not allowed here. Please _____ your cigarettes.

   B: Sure. I'll put _____ away right now.

3. A: The movie is over. Would you please _____ the VCR?

   B: Sure. I'll turn _____ off right now.

4. A: It's dark in here. Would you please _____ the lights?

   B: Sure. I'll turn _____ on right away.

5. A: It's too hot in here. Please _____ the heat.

   B: Sure. I'll turn _____ down right away.

6. A: My car won't start. Could you please _____ me _____?

   B: OK. I'll pick _____ up in thirty minutes.

Small Talk

Practice this conversation with a partner.

A: Would you please *clean up the work area?*

B: Sure. I'll *clean it up* right away.

1. turn off that machine

2. give back my screwdriver

3. put on your goggles

4. call back Mr. Davis

5. put away your tools

Partnerwork

▶ Person A

Person A looks at this page only. Person B looks at page 124 only. You and your partner have the same list of things to do from yesterday. A check mark (✓) means that item is already done.

Ask your partner questions to find out the things he or she did yesterday. Then look at the check marks on your list and answer your partner's questions.

Example: A: Did you *call up your friend* yesterday?

B: Yes, I *called her up in the morning.*

OR No, I forgot to *call her up.*

OR No, I didn't have time to *call her up.*

Things to Do

   call up my friend
✓ clean up the apartment
✓ give back Peter's books
   put away my clothes
✓ pick up my suit at the dry cleaner's
   find out about a visa for Ecuador

Person B looks at this page only. Person A looks at page 123 only. You and your partner have the same list of things to do from yesterday. A check mark (✓) means that item is already done.

Look at the check marks on your list and answer your partner's questions. Then ask your partner the same questions and check what he or she did yesterday.

Example: A: Did you *call up your friend* yesterday?
       B: Yes, I *called her up in the morning.*
         OR No, I forgot to *call her up.*
         OR No, I didn't have time to *call her up.*

Things to Do

✓ call up my friend
   clean up the apartment
   give back Peter's books
✓ put away my clothes
   pick up my suit at the dry cleaner's
✓ find out about a visa for Ecuador

Wrapping Up

Make your own list of six things you needed to do yesterday. You had time to do some of the things but not all of them. Choose verbs from the list or add your own. Exchange lists with a partner. Find out which things your partner did.

Things to Do   **Two-Word Verbs**

1. _____   call up
                                  call back
2. _____   call off
                                  clean up
3. _____   find out
                                  give back
4. _____   give up
                                  look up
5. _____   pick up
                                  put away
6. _____   write down

Unit 14 What should they do?

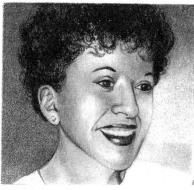

Maria: I plan to learn about computers.

Ramón: I want to be a good father.

Carlos: I want to become a good soccer player.

Rita: My goal is to own a clothing store.

Magda: One of my goals is to save enough money for Martin's college education.

Martin: My most important goal is to go to college.

Hanh: My goal is to buy a house.

Nam: I want to bring my brother to the United States.

An: I want to teach my grandchildren about Vietnam.

A goal is something you want to do in the future. What is one of your goals?

Setting the Scene

Rita wants to own a clothing store some day. She asked her family and friends for advice. Here it is:

Rita: My goal is to own a clothing store.

Ramón: You should take some business courses.

Maria: You should work for a while in a clothing store. Then you can learn about the business first.

Hanh: You could go into business with a friend.

Magda: You'd better save a lot of money first!

Should

You **should** take some business courses.

| I
You
He
She
We
You
They | **should** save some money. |

> We use *should* to tell what we think is the best way to do something. We often use *should* to give advice or express an opinion.

 1 Do you agree or disagree with the advice of Rita's family and friends? Check Agree or Disagree.

Rita's goal: She wants to own a clothing store.

Advice	Agree	Disagree
She should take some business courses.	____	____
She should work in a store first.	____	____
She should save some money.	____	____
She should go into business with a friend.	____	____

2 What other advice do you have for Rita? List your ideas.

1. _She should_ _____

2. _____

3 Work in a group. What should Martin do to reach his goal? Check Very important, Useful, or Not important.

Martin's goal: He wants to go to college.

Advice	Very important	Useful	Not important
He should study hard in high school.	____	____	____
He should get good grades.	____	____	____
He should make a lot of friends.	____	____	____
He should read a lot.	____	____	____
He should learn to play a musical instrument.	____	____	____
He should join a sports team.	____	____	____
He should get a job.	____	____	____
He should learn a second language.	____	____	____

4 Work with a partner. Answer the question below. Write your ideas in the blank circles. Share your ideas with the class.

What should Ramón do to reach his goal?

Could

> Rita:　I want to earn more money now. What should I do?
>
> Magda:　Well, you **could** work longer hours. Or you **could** get a second
> job. You **could** work in the evening at a restaurant or a store.
> But you should think about it carefully. You can't work all day
> and all night. You'll get sick.
>
> We use *could* to suggest possible solutions. The meaning of *should* is
> stronger than *could*.

5　List three of your goals.

1. _____
2. _____
3. _____

**6　Write one of your goals below. Exchange books with a partner.
Have your partner write two suggestions with *could* in your
book. Repeat with two more students.**

Goal: _____

What should I do to reach my goal?

Your Classmates' Suggestions

Student 1: _____

　　　　OR _____

Student 2: _____

　　　　OR _____

Student 3: _____

　　　　OR _____

7 **Give your advice or suggestions. Use *should* or *could*.**

1. Richard wants to learn Spanish. What should he do?

_____

2. Mario wants to make American friends. What should he do?

_____

3. Angela wants to quit smoking. What should she do?

_____

4. Ana is a newcomer to the U.S. She is living far away from her family and friends. She often feels lonely. What should she do?

_____

Shouldn't

You **shouldn't** quit school.
You **shouldn't** smoke.

I	**shouldn't** smoke.
You	
He	
She	
We	
You	
They	

Contraction:
should not
⤵
shouldn't

> Use *shouldn't* to give advice or express an opinion about what not to do.

8 **What do you think? Check Agree or Disagree. Choose one opinion and explain why you agree or disagree.**

Opinion	Agree	Disagree
1. People shouldn't get married before they are 20.	____	____
2. People with children shouldn't get divorced.	____	____
3. Parents shouldn't spank their children.	____	____
4. Children shouldn't watch TV on school nights.	____	____
5. Women shouldn't work outside the home.	____	____
6. Men shouldn't cry.	____	____
7. Men shouldn't baby-sit.	____	____

Practice this conversation with a partner.

A: You shouldn't *smoke.*
B: Why not?
A: Because *it's bad for your health.*

1. smoke/it's bad for your health

2. quit school/you won't get a good job

3. quit your job/you won't have enough money

4. buy a car/cars are too expensive

5. _____/_____

9 Think of things you should or shouldn't do in these places. Tell a classmate.

10 Work with a partner. Read about these problems. Write your advice. Use *should, shouldn't,* or *could.*

1. I like to go out on weekends. I really enjoy dancing and visiting friends. My husband doesn't like to go out on weekends. He wants to stay at home. Every weekend we argue about this. What should we do?

   _____

   _____

   _____

2. My daughter is 17 years old. She is dating a 25-year-old man right now. I think he is too old for her. What should I do?

   _____

   _____

3. I just arrived in the United States with my wife and four children. Right now we are living in a very small apartment with my brother and his family. It's very crowded. Soon I hope to find a cheap apartment nearby. But how do you find an apartment in the U.S.? What should I do? _____

   _____

   _____

Advice on Aches and Pains

What should these people do? Choose an idea from the list or use your own.

Roger has a **headache**.
Andrew has a **stomachache**.
Philip has **an earache**.
Peter has a **bad cough**.
Sam has a **fever**.

He should drink some warm milk.
He should drink some water.
He should get some rest.
He should take some Tylenol.
He should take some cough medicine.
He should stay in bed.

Had better

Rita has a fever of 104°F and a very sore throat. She **had better** go to the doctor.

I	**had better** go to the doctor.	I'd	**better** go to the doctor.
You		You'd	
He		He'd	
She		She'd	
We		We'd	
You		You'd	
They		They'd	

Had better expresses urgent advice or a strong opinion.

Contraction:
She had better
∨
She'd better

11 Listen to these conversations. What advice does Magda give to her friends? Write her advice below. Use her exact words.

1. _____

2. _____

3. _____

12 Complete these conversations. Then practice them with a partner.

1. A: Are you going to the party?
   B: Well, I want to, but I have a terrible headache.
   A: Really? You'd better _____.

2. A: Are you OK?
   B: No. I have a horrible stomachache. I can't even stand up straight.
   A: You'd better _____.

3. A: Did you take your medicine?
   B: No, I forgot to.
   A: You forgot? Well, you'd better _____.

4. A: Did you make a doctor's appointment?
   B: No, I forgot to.
   A: You'd better _____.

Use What You Know

Work in a group. Choose one of the problems below. What should people with this problem do? List ideas from your classmates. Write sentences with *could*, *should*, or *had better*. Then share your ideas with the class.

a toothache	a sore throat	a backache
a minor burn	a nosebleed	the hiccups

Problem: _____

Advice: _____

_____

_____

_____

_____

Wrapping Up

What advice do you have for newcomers to the United States? Write your ideas below. Then compare ideas with your classmates. Use your ideas to make a class-information booklet for newcomers to the United States.

_____

_____

_____

_____

Unit 15 Have you ever worked in a store?

Rita hopes to get a job in a clothing store. What questions do you think the manager will ask her?

Setting the Scene

This job advertisement appeared in the newspaper. Rita called and made an appointment for an interview.

> Available immediately. Openings for Store Clerks, full time, must be dependable, experience preferred, call Mon-Fri, noon-4 p.m. at 542-3493.

At the job interview, Rita talked to the manager of the store. Here is part of their conversation:

Manager:	Have you ever worked in a store?
Rita:	Yes, I have. I worked in my uncle's jewelry store in Puerto Rico.
Manager:	Oh, I see. Did you like the work?
Rita:	Yes, very much. I like to be busy, and there's always something to learn in a store.
Manager:	That's for sure! Have you ever worked in a clothing store?
Rita:	No, I haven't. But I'm eager to learn about it.
Manager:	Why is that?
Rita:	Well, I want to have my own store someday.

Present Perfect with *Ever*

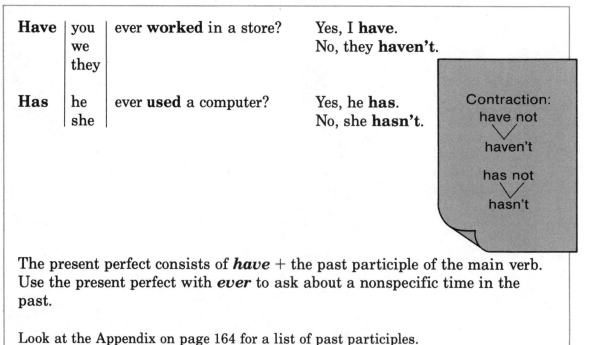

Have	you we they	ever **worked** in a store?	Yes, I **have**. No, they **haven't**.
Has	he she	ever **used** a computer?	Yes, he **has**. No, she **hasn't**.

Contraction:
have not ⌄ haven't

has not ⌄ hasn't

The present perfect consists of **have** + the past participle of the main verb. Use the present perfect with **ever** to ask about a nonspecific time in the past.

Look at the Appendix on page 164 for a list of past participles.

1 Answer these questions. Check Yes, I have or No, I haven't.

	Yes, I have.	No, I haven't.
1. Have you ever worked in a store?	——	——
2. Have you ever worked in a hospital?	——	——
3. Have you ever worked in a restaurant?	——	——
4. Have you ever worked in a factory?	——	——
5. Have you ever worked in an office?	——	——
6. Have you ever traveled by train?	——	——
7. Have you ever traveled by plane?	——	——
8. Have you ever traveled by bus?	——	——

Use these questions to interview your teacher.

Small Talk

Practice this conversation with a partner.

A: Have you ever used *a computer*?
B: Yes, I have.
A: Can you show me how to use one?
B: Sure. I'd be glad to.

1. a computer

2. a copier

3. a fax machine

4. an ATM

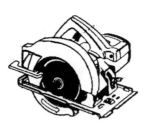

5. an electric saw

6. jumper cables

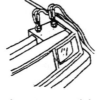
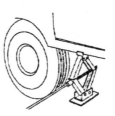

7. a car jack

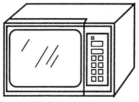

8. a microwave oven

Irregular Verbs

Have you ever **eaten** Japanese food?   Yes, I have.
Have you ever **gone** to Japan?   No, I haven't.

Many verbs have an irregular past participle. Some examples are:

buy—bought	make—made
drive—driven	ride—ridden
eat—eaten	see—seen
give—given	take—taken
go—gone	write—written

Look at the Appendix on page 164 for a list of past participles of irregular verbs.

2 **Work with a partner. Take turns asking and answering questions about your experiences. Use the present perfect.**

Example: A: Have you ever *eaten Japanese food?*
    B: *No, I haven't.* Have you?
    A: *Yes, I have.*

1. eat Japanese food
2. eat Colombian food
3. take a train
4. go to Mexico
5. go to Haiti
6. go to Canada

7. ride a motorcycle
8. drive a truck
9. see a volcano
10. give a surprise party
11. make a birthday cake
12. write a poem

Ask a different classmate about his or her partner.

Example: A: Has Marek ever *eaten Japanese food?*
    B: Yes, he has. OR No, he hasn't.

Present Perfect and Simple Past

A: Have you ever worked in a store?
B: Yes, I have. I worked in my uncle's store last year.
A: Did you work there full-time?
B: Yes, I did.

Use the present perfect to ask about a nonspecific time in the past. Use the simple past to tell about a specific time in the past.

3 Complete this conversation. Use *ever, last, ago,* or *from . . . to*.

A: Have you _____ worked in a restaurant?

B: Yes, I have. I worked at The Happy Wok restaurant _____ 1990 _____ 1993. I also worked at a restaurant in my country six years _____.

A: Are you working now?

B: No. I left my job _____ year because I wanted to study full time.

A: Have you finished your studies?

B: Yes, I have. I graduated two weeks _____.

4 Look at your Yes answers from Exercise 1. Give specific information about the place and the time. Use the simple past.

Example: I worked in a grocery store in my country four years ago.

1. _____

2. _____

3. _____

5 Try to find someone who has worked in each place. Ask your classmates. Write the information in the chart.

Example: José: Ana, have you worked in *a store*?
Ana: No, I haven't.
José: Miguel, have you worked in *a store*?
Miguel: Yes, I have. I worked in a grocery store in Mexico five years ago.

Report to the class:

José: Miguel worked in a grocery store in Mexico five years ago.

Place	Classmate's Name	Where	When
1. a store	_____	_____	_____
2. a hospital	_____	_____	_____
3. a restaurant	_____	_____	_____
4. a factory	_____	_____	_____
5. an office	_____	_____	_____

6 Turn to the U.S. map on page 168. Where have you gone in the United States? Put a check mark on those states. Then talk to a classmate about one of those states.

Examples:

A: Have you ever gone to California?
B: Yes, I have. I went there last year.
A: What did you do there?
B: I visited my brother.

A: Have you ever gone to Florida?
B: No, I haven't. Have you?
A: Yes, I went there last year.
B: What did you do there?
A: I visited my friends.

7 Make a class list of popular foods in your native countries. Choose a food that is new to you from the list on the board. Then find someone who has eaten this food and ask about it.

Example: fried rice
A: Have you ever eaten *fried rice*?
B: Yes, I have.
A: What's in it?
B: It has *rice, vegetables, and spices* in it.

Focus on Vocabulary

Tips for Job Hunting

Read these tips and circle the two-word verbs.

- Look over the Help Wanted ads in the newspaper.
- Call your friends up. They might know about a job opening.
- Fill out job application forms carefully. Write clearly and answer every question.
- Look over your job application form before you give it back. Correct any mistakes.
- You don't have to accept a job. If the working conditions are unsafe, turn the job down.

What do you think the two-word verbs mean? Use the words and ideas around the verb to guess.

Can you think of other job-hunting tips?

8 Complete these conversations. Use a two-word verb from the list.

call up   fill out   look over   turn down

1. A: Did you _____ your application?

    B: Yes, and I found a few mistakes.

2. A: Did you _____ the job ads in the newspaper?

    B: Yes, but I didn't find anything.

3. A: Would you please _____ this form?

    B: Sure. Should I use a pen or a pencil?

    A: A pen will be fine.

4. A: Did you get the job?

    B: They offered it to me, but I'm going to _____ it _____.

    A: Why?

    B: Because the pay is too low.

5. A: You could _____ your friends. They might know
        about a job.

    B: That's a good idea. I will.

Must

Rules	Laws
You **must** be quiet in a hospital.	Children **must** go to school.
You **must** get to school on time.	You **must** be 16 years old to get a driver's license.
	You **must** be a U.S. citizen to vote.

Requirements

Office Position
Full-time for busy office. **Must** have good computer and telephone skills.

Immediate Openings
Auto technician. **Must** have own tools and transportation.

Use *must* to talk about rules, laws, and requirements.

9 Think about these jobs in the U.S. Are these requirements true or false? Check True or False. Compare your answers in small groups.

Police Officer	True	False
1. You must have a driver's license.	___	___
2. You must be tall.	___	___
3. You must be older than 25.	___	___
4. You must be a U.S. citizen.	___	___
Teacher		
1. You must have a college education.	___	___
2. You must have a driver's license.	___	___
3. You must be younger than 50.	___	___
Post Office Employee		
1. You must pass an examination.	___	___
2. You must be a man.	___	___
3. You must have a college education.	___	___
4. You must be able to read.	___	___
5. You must be a U.S. citizen.	___	___

10 Look in the Help Wanted section of a newspaper. Find a job ad that interests you. Tell your classmates about the job but don't identify it. Let your classmates guess the job. (Save this ad for later.)

Must Not

You **must not** smoke here.
You **must not** drink this. It's poison.

Must not is different from *don't have to*. *Don't have to* means "It's OK, but it's not necessary."
You **don't have to** drink orange juice every day.
You **must not** drink alcohol and drive.

Must not means "It is not allowed."

11 What do these signs mean? Use *must* or *must not* in your answers.

Example: *You must not drive faster than the speed limit.*

  ONE WAY

SPEED LIMIT **55**   DO NOT ENTER   DO NOT PASS   ONE WAY   NO TURN ON RED

12 Complete these sentences. Use *must not* or *don't have to.*

1. Children _____ play with matches.

2. Children _____ have bicycles.

3. Parents _____ leave babies at home alone.

4. Parents _____ buy expensive toys for their children.

5. Parents _____ let their children play with real guns.

6. Children _____ do homework on Friday night.

7. Parents _____ abuse their children.

8. Parents _____ videotape their children.

9. Children under six _____ go to school.

10. Children _____ eat apples.

13 Work with a group of classmates. What are some rules in these situations? Write your ideas. Use *must* or *must not.*

Riding a bus

_____

_____

_____

Driving a car

_____

_____

_____

Working in an office

_____

_____

_____

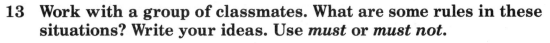

14 **Listen to this job interview and answer the questions. Write short answers.**

    1. Has Lisa ever worked in an office?

    _____

    2. When did she work in the office?

    _____

    3. Why did she leave?

    _____

In Your Own Words

Use the job ad you chose for Exercise 10. Think of questions someone might ask at an interview for this job. Write your questions on a separate piece of paper.

Examples: Have you ever worked in a hospital?
                Did you like the work?
                When did you work there?
                Do you want to work full-time or part-time?

Wrapping Up

Work with a partner. Role-play one of these situations.

A. Role-play a job interview. Add your own questions.

Manager: How do you do? (*Shakes hands.*) My name is _____.
Applicant: My name is _____. It's nice to meet you.
Manager: Please have a seat.
Applicant: Thank you.
Manager: I understand that you are looking for a job as a _____.
Applicant: Yes, that's correct.
Manager: Have you ever _____?
Applicant: _____

B. Role-play a conversation between two friends who meet by chance on the street.

A: Hi, _____. How are you?
B: Fine. And you?
A: I'm pretty good. I'm just on my way to _____ (store/restaurant). Have you ever been there?
B: _____

1 Read this paragraph about getting married in the U.S.

To get married in the United States, you must get a marriage license. In some states, you have to be 18 years old to get this license. A person younger than 18 must have parental permission to get married. After you get your license, you must find someone to perform the marriage ceremony. This person might be a justice of the peace or a minister.

Read these statements and circle TRUE or FALSE.

1. A 16-year-old can't get married in the U.S. TRUE FALSE

2. People under 18 must have permission from their parents to get married in the U.S. TRUE FALSE

3. An 18-year-old doesn't have to have parental permission to get married. TRUE FALSE

4. You must be 18 to get married in the U.S. TRUE FALSE

5. An 18-year-old doesn't have to get a marriage license. TRUE FALSE

6. You might go to a justice of the peace to get married. TRUE FALSE

2 What must you do to get married in your native country? Tell your classmates.

3 What's your opinion? Circle YES, NO, or MAYBE. Then compare answers with a partner.

1. A couple should live together before they get married. YES NO MAYBE

2. People should be at least 21 years old before they get married. YES NO MAYBE

3. Married couples shouldn't have children for several years. YES NO MAYBE

4. Parents should choose a husband or wife for their children. YES NO MAYBE

5. Husbands should be older than their wives. YES NO MAYBE

4 Work in small groups. What advice do you have for newlyweds? List your ideas. Then make a class list.

5 Work with a partner. Check who should do these chores.

Who should . . . ?	Husband only	Wife only	Both husband and wife
cook the meals clean up the kitchen discipline the children buy the groceries put away the groceries mend the clothes earn the money pay the bills make decisions			

6 Do you like to do these chores?

7 Listen to this poem. Then read it aloud several times.

My Rules

If you want to marry me, here's what you'll have to do:
You must learn how to make a perfect chicken-dumpling stew.
And you must sew my holey socks,
And soothe my troubled mind,
And develop the knack for scratching my back,
And keep my shoes spotlessly shined.
And while I rest you must rake up the leaves,
And when it is hailing and snowing
You must shovel the walk . . . and be still when I talk,
And—hey—where are you going?

—Shel Silverstein

8 Work in groups. Read the poem again and answer these questions. Share your answers with the class.
1. Do you think the speaker is a man or a woman? Why?
2. What happens at the end of the poem? Why?
3. Complete this sentence: If you want to marry me, you must

_____.

Review: Units 13–15

Teacher Script for Listening Exercises

Unit 1

Page 3

Exercise 3

1. Man: Fariba, do you get up early on Saturday?
   Woman: On Saturday? No, I don't. I get up late.
2. Man: Do you work on Saturday?
   Woman: No, I don't. I work on Monday, Wednesday, and Friday. But I don't work on Saturday.
3. Man: Do you go to school on Saturday?
   Woman: Yes, I do.
4. Man: Do you study English at school?
   Woman: No, I don't. I study math.
5. Man: Do you go shopping on Saturday?
   Woman: No, I don't.

Unit 3

Page 20

Exercise 1

1. Please bring your book to class.
2. Put the dishes over here.
3. Write your stories for tomorrow.
4. Ask the man for directions.

Unit 4

Page 37

Exercise 9

1. Woman: Pierre, where were you last night?
   Man: At home. I was sick.
   Woman: That's too bad.
2. Teenage Boy: Sonya, were you at the basketball game last night?
   Teenage Girl: No, I was at work.
   Teenage Boy: That's too bad. It was a great game.
3. Woman: The video store was really busy last night.
   Man: I know. I was there at 8 o'clock.

Unit 5

Page 40

Exercise 1

1. They talk a lot.
2. They called us.

3. They watched a lot of TV.
4. They play at the park.
5. They asked a lot of questions.

Page 42

Exercise 4

1. Woman: Hi. Is Maria there?
   Man: No. I'm sorry. She's not here right now.
   Woman: Oh. Well, please tell her Mrs. Rogers called.
   Man: Sure. Anything else?
   Woman: Ask her to call me at 837-9045.
   Man: Sure.
   Woman: Thanks. Good-bye.
   Man: Good-bye.

2. Woman: Hello. Is Maria there?
   Man: No, she's not here right now. Can I take a message?
   Woman: Well, yes. This is Mrs. Gonzalez. Just tell her I talked to Carlos and everything is fine.
   Man: Okay. I'll tell her.
   Woman: Thanks very much. Good-bye.
   Man: Good-bye.

Unit 7

Page 67

Exercise 13

1. Ron's beard is shorter than mine.
2. Ron's nose is smaller than mine.
3. Ron's hair is curlier than mine.
4. Ron's hair is longer than mine.
5. Ron's glasses are bigger than mine.

Unit 9

Page 82

Exercise 8

1. Jean is the tallest.
2. Philip is the oldest.
3. Ali is the youngest.
4. Mario is the shortest.
5. Dan is the heaviest.
6. Robert is the thinnest.

Exercise 9

1. Who's the tallest person in the class?
2. Whose book is on your desk?
3. Whose pencil is this?

4. Who's your best friend?
5. Who's sitting on your right?
6. Whose grandmother is this?

Unit 10

Page 90
Exercise 7
1. Do you have to work tomorrow, Ramón?
   No, tomorrow's Saturday. I'm going to stay home.
2. François, do you need the car tomorrow?
   Yes, I do. I have to go to work.
3. Nam, do you have to go to work tomorrow?
   No, I don't have to work on Saturday.
4. Hanh, what are you going to do tomorrow?
   Tomorrow's Saturday. I have to work.

Page 92
Exercise 10
1. I can swim.
2. She can't speak Spanish.
3. He can't play the guitar.
4. We can dance.
5. They can type fast.
6. I can't lift 100 pounds.

Unit 11

Page 98
Exercise 1
1. I walk fast.
2. He'll drink coffee.
3. She'll drive to work.
4. We do our best.
5. You work hard.
6. They'll ride the bus to school.

Page 102
Exercise 9
1. What are you doing?
2. Where are you going to go?
3. Can you speak Spanish?
4. How long will it take you to get there?
5. Did you go there last year?

Exercise 10
Maria: What are you doing, Rita?
 Rita: Planning a trip.
Maria: Did you call Laura?
 Rita: Not yet. I'll call her in a minute.

Exercise 11
Laura: Where are you going, Rita?
 Rita: To the passport office.
Laura: Did you get a passport photo?
 Rita: Yes, I did.
Laura: Good. Are we going to meet at the restaurant?
 Rita: Yes. I'll be there at six o'clock.

Unit 12

Page 107
Exercise 4
1. Are you going to go to Rita's house this afternoon?
   I'm not sure. I might.
2. Tina, are you going to do the dishes?
   Sure, Mom. I'll do them later.
3. Where are you going to eat lunch?
   I don't know. I might eat at Sam's house.
4. Are you going to go to the dance?
   I plan to.
   Can you give me a ride?
   Sure. I'll pick you up at 7 o'clock.

Unit 14

Page 131
Exercise 11
1. Magda: How are you today?
    Hanh: Well, I have a very bad toothache.
   Magda: Oh, you'd better see a dentist. Do you have one?
    Hanh: Yes, thanks.
2. Magda: Do you feel better today?
    Maria: No. I still have a sore throat.
   Magda: That's too bad. You'd better stay home today. Do you need anything?
    Maria: No, thanks.
3. Magda: How's Rita doing?
    Maria: She still has a bad cough. I'm worried about her.
   Magda: It might be serious. She'd better go to the doctor.
    Maria: I think so. I'll make an appointment right away.

Unit 15

Page 142
Exercise 14
Manager: Have you ever worked in an office?
   Lisa: Yes, I have. I worked in the business office of City Hospital.
Manager: Oh, I see. When did you work there?
   Lisa: Two years ago.
Manager: Why did you leave?
   Lisa: I decided to go back to school.

Teacher Script

Appendix

Syllables
Page 151
Exercise 5

1. apple	5. grandfather
2. table	6. lunch
3. cake	7. sisters
4. father	8. pineapple

Pronunciation of Plural Nouns
Page 153
Exercise 2

1. spoons	6. houses
2. dollars	7. toys
3. matches	8. months
4. slices	9. ounces
5. names	

Pronunciation of the Simple Past
Page 157
Exercise 2

1. looked	6. worked
2. watched	7. closed
3. started	8. waited
4. lived	9. invited
5. added	

Appendix

Spelling of the Simple Present

Third-Person Singular Spelling Rules	Examples
1. To make the third person singular, add -s to the simple form of most verbs.	He works. She works. It works. He sings. She sings. It sings. He eats. She eats. It eats.
2. Add -es to the simple form of verbs that end in these letters: s, z, sh, ch, and x.	He misses. She misses. It misses. He washes. She washes. It washes. He watches. She watches. It watches.
3. For verbs that end in a consonant before -y, change the y to i and add -es.	He studies. She studies. He worries. She worries. He tries. She tries. It tries.
4. Have, do, and go have special forms.	He has. She has. It has. He does. She does. It does. He goes. She goes. It goes.

1 **Fill in the blanks with the correct form of the verb. Use the simple present.**

Mae-Ning ___wants___ (*want*) to be a computer programmer.

She ___goes___ (*go*) to Portland Community College. She ___He has___ (*have*) classes four nights a week. She ___likes___ (*like*) her classes, and she ___studies___ (*study*) very hard.

She ___has___ (*have*) a full-time job during the day. She ___works___ (*work*) at a preschool. She ___teaches___ (*teach*) the children songs, and she ___plays___ (*play*) with them.

She ___likes___ (*like*) her busy schedule.

Spelling of *-ing* Forms

Spelling Rules	Examples
1. Add *-ing* to the simple form of most verbs to form the present continuous.	eat—eat**ing** cook—cook**ing** try—try**ing**
2. If the simple form of the verb ends in *-e*, drop the *-e*. Then add *-ing*.	write—writ**ing** make—mak**ing** live—liv**ing**
3. If the simple form of the verb is one syllable, and it ends in consonant + vowel + consonant, double the final consonant. Then add *-ing*.	sit—sit**ting** get—get**ting** run—run**ning** stop—stop**ping** put—put**ting**

1 **Fill in the blanks with the correct form of the verb. Use the present continuous.**

1. Ramón is very busy in the morning. Right now he _is_ _getting_ (*get*) ready for work. He _is_ _shaving_ (*shave*). He _is_ _trying_ (*try*) to get to work on time.

2. Maria's family is very busy in the evening. Right now Maria _is_ _cooking_ (*cook*) dinner. She _is_ _making_ (*make*) a special dessert. Her baby _is_ _sitting_ (*sit*) in his high chair. He _is_ _crying_ (*cry*). Tina and Juanita _are_ _doing_ (*do*) their homework. Carlos _is_ _writing_ (*write*) a letter to his grandmother. Ramón _is_ _putting_ (*put*) some plates on the table.

Syllables

In English, words have one, two, three, or more separate parts that you can hear. Listen to your teacher say these words:

dish
1

dish es
1   2

dish wash er
1   2   3

(1 syllable)   (2 syllables)   (3 syllables)

1 Words with one syllable have one part. Listen to your teacher say these words. Listen again and repeat them.

1. dish   2. egg   3. boy   4. girl   5. man
   1   1   1   1   1

2 Words with two syllables have two parts. Listen to your teacher say these words. Listen again and repeat them.

1. dishes   2. lady   3. baby   4. mother   5. sandwich
   1 2   1 2   1 2   1   2   1   2

3 Words with three syllables have three parts. Listen to your teacher say these words. Listen again and repeat.

1. tomato   2. potato   3. banana   4. sandwiches
   1   2 3   1 2 3   1 2 3   1   2 3

4 Listen and repeat these words. Tap on your desk one time for each syllable that you hear.

1. cheese   2. pear   3. peach   4. dish

5. grape   6. lemon   7. coffee   8. peaches

9. dishes   10. table   11. boxes   12. dishwasher

13. sandwiches   14. tablecloth   15. hamburger   16. grandmother

5 Your teacher will read some words. Write them down. Then write the number of syllables next to each word.

1. _apple_ 2
2. _boxes_ 2
3. _ _____ _ 1
4. _ _____ _ 2

5. _mother_ 2
6. _egrape_ 1
7. _eggto_ 1
8. _tomato_ 3

6 How many syllables are in your name? Write each syllable below. Add more lines if you need them.

Example: First Name: Maria   Last Name: Sánchez
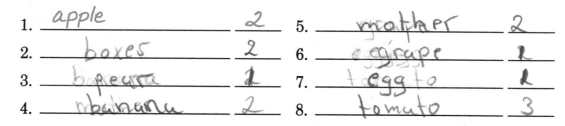
              1 23   1   2

First Name

_LS_	_uL_	_____	_____	_____	_____
1	2	3	4	5	6

Last Name

_____	_____	_____	_____	_____	_____
1	2	3	4	5	6

7 Work with a partner. Say your first and last name. Your partner will tap on the desk the number of syllables in your name. Was your partner correct? Take turns.

Pronunciation of Plural Nouns

To make the plural form of most nouns, add an /s/* sound or a /z/ sound to them. Do not say an extra syllable when you say these plural nouns. (But we always write an -s.)

Examples:

/s/ sound	/z/ sound
grape—grapes	cab—cabs
cat—cats	dad—dads
book—books	egg—eggs
student—students	boy—boys
month—months	teacher—teachers
	name—names

Do add an extra syllable when the noun ends in these sounds:

Sound	Singular—Plural	Singular—Plural
/s/	class—classes 1 1 2	price—prices 1 1 2
/z/	size—sizes 1 1 2	nose—noses (s = /z/) 1 1 2
/sh/	dish—dishes 1 1 2	wish—wishes 1 1 2
/zh/	garage—garages 1 2 1 2 3	corsage—corsages 1 2 1 2 3
/ch/	watch—watches 1 1 2	lunch—lunches 1 1 2
/j/	page—pages 1 1 2	language—languages 1 2 1 2 3
/ks/	box—boxes 1 1 2	tax—taxes 1 1 2

1 **Repeat these words and sentences after your teacher. These plural nouns do not have an extra syllable.**

1. grapes   The grapes are delicious.
2. pounds   I need two pounds of cheese.
3. teachers   The teachers are happy.
4. students   The students are busy.
5. keys   Where are my keys?

*We use slashes to talk about sounds. The letter inside the slashes tells the sound.

2 **Listen to your teacher say some plural words. Is there an extra syllable? Check the correct box.**

1. ☑ no extra syllable
   ☐ extra syllable

2. ☐ no extra syllable
   ☑ extra syllable

3. ☑ no extra syllable
   ☐ extra syllable

4. ☑ no extra syllable
   ☐ extra syllable

5. ☐ no extra syllable
   ☑ extra syllable

6. ☑ no extra syllable
   ☐ extra syllable

7. ☐ no extra syllable
   ☑ extra syllable

8. ☑ no extra syllable
   ☐ extra syllable

9. ☐ no extra syllable
   ☑ extra syllable

3 **Listen and repeat these words and sentences after your teacher. These noun plurals have an extra syllable.**

1. taxes
   1 2

   Taxes are high in this state.
   1 2

2. prices
   1 2

   The prices are good at this store.
   —1 2

3. buses
   1 2

   The buses are late today.
   1 2

4. roses
   1 2

   The roses are beautiful!
   1 2

5. languages
   1   2   3

   How many languages do you speak?
   1   2   3

4 **Work with a partner. One person reads the words in Column One aloud. Then the other person reads the words in Column Two aloud. Decide together which words have an extra syllable and which ones do not. Write *yes* or *no* after each word.**

Column One	Extra Syllable?	Column Two	Extra Syllable?
1. tables	yes	1. sandwiches	yes
2. suitcases	yes	2. sales	no
3. watches	yes	3. nurses	yes
4. gloves	no	4. workers	no
5. ropes	no	5. friends	no

Spelling of Plural Nouns

Spelling Rules	Examples
1. Add -s to most singular nouns.	fork—forks, boy—boys, price—prices, nose—noses
2. Add -es to nouns that end in these letters: s, z, sh, ch, and x.	glass—glasses, dish—dishes, inch—inches, box—boxes
3. When the simple form ends in -y after a consonant, change the y to i and add -es.	baby—babies, lady—ladies, party—parties, berry—berries
4. When the simple form ends in -o after a consonant, add -es.[1]	tomato—tomatoes, potato—potatoes
5. For nouns that end in -f or -fe, change the -f or -fe to -ves.[2]	leaf—leaves, knife—knives, shelf—shelves
6. There are also some irregular nouns. Here are some common ones.	person—**people**, man—**men**, woman—**women**, child—child**ren**, foot—**feet**, tooth—**teeth**, mouse—**mice**, goose—**geese**

1 Write the plural form of these nouns.

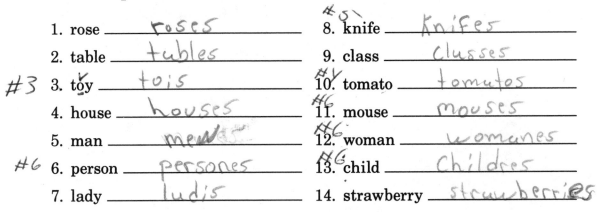

1. rose _____ roses _____
2. table _____ tables _____
#3 3. toy _____ tois _____
4. house _____ houses _____
5. man _____ mews _____
#6 6. person _____ persones _____
7. lady _____ ludis _____

#5 8. knife _____ knifes _____
9. class _____ clusses _____
#4 10. tomato _____ tomutos _____
#6 11. mouse _____ mouses _____
#6 12. woman _____ womanes _____
#6 13. child _____ childres _____
14. strawberry _____ strawberries _____

[1]There are some exceptions to this rule (e.g., piano—pianos).
[2]There are some exceptions to this rule (e.g., chief—chiefs).

Weights and Measures

Weight

Units: ounce, pound, ton

16 ounces (oz.) = 1 pound (lb.)
2,000 pounds = 1 ton (tn.)

Liquid and Dry

Units: fluid ounce, cup, pint, quart, gallon
teaspoon, tablespoon

8 fluid ounces = 1 cup (c.)
2 cups (c.) = 1 pint (pt.)
2 pints = 1 quart (qt.)
4 quarts = 1 gallon (gal.)
3 teaspoons (tsp.) = 1 tablespoon (tbsp.)

Distance

Units: inch, foot, yard, mile

12 inches (in.) = 1 foot (ft.)
3 feet = 1 yard (yd.)
1,760 yards = 1 mile (mi.)

Pronunciation of the Simple Past

When we say the simple past form of most verbs, we add a /t/ or a /d/ sound to them. We do not say an extra syllable when we say the past form. (When we write the simple past form, it always ends in *-ed*.)

Examples:

/t/ sound	/d/ sound
stop—stopped 1 1	rob—robbed 1 1
look—looked 1 1	wave—waved 1 1
watch—watched 1 1	play—played 1 1

We do add an extra syllable when the simple form of the verb ends in a *t* or *d* sound.

Examples:

wait—waited 1 1 2	need—needed 1 1 2
want—wanted 1 1 2	decide—decided 1 2 1 2 3

1 **Listen and repeat these words and sentences after your teacher. These past tense verbs do not have an extra syllable.**

1. packed   I packed my suitcase last night.
    1   1

2. washed   They washed the dishes.
    1   1

3. talked   Peter talked for an hour.
    1   1

4. watched   We watched a movie yesterday.
    1   1

5. played   They played in the park.
    1   1

6. rained   It rained last night.
    1   1

7. called   My sister called yesterday.
    1   1

2 **Listen to your teacher say some past tense verbs. Is there an extra syllable? Check the correct box.**

1. □ no extra syllable 2. □ no extra syllable 3. □ no extra syllable
   □ extra syllable   □ extra syllable   □ extra syllable

4. □ no extra syllable 5. □ no extra syllable 6. □ no extra syllable
   □ extra syllable   □ extra syllable   □ extra syllable

7. □ no extra syllable 8. □ no extra syllable 9. □ no extra syllable
   □ extra syllable   □ extra syllable   □ extra syllable

3 **Listen and repeat these words and sentences after your teacher. These simple past verbs have an extra syllable.**

1. waited   I waited for my friend.
     1 2   1 2

2. wanted   Carlos wanted to go home.
     1 2   1 2

'3. needed   Maria needed some information.
     1 2   1 2

4. decided   Ramón decided to stay home.
     1 2 3   1 2 3

5. invited   Rita invited her friends to a party.
     1 2 3   1 2 3

6. started   The movie started late.
     1 2   1 2

4 **Work with a partner. One person reads the words in Column One aloud. Then the other person reads the words in Column Two aloud. Decide together which words have an extra syllable and which ones do not. Write *yes* or *no* after each word.**

Column One	Extra Syllable?	Column Two	Extra Syllable?
1. watched	no	1. asked	no
2. looked	no	2. started	yes
3. waited	yes	3. wished	no
4. liked	no	4. invited	yes
5. added	yes	5. opened	no
6. lived	no	6. worked	no
7. needed	yes	7. decided	yes

Simple Past (Irregular Verbs)

Here are some of the more common irregular verbs and their simple past forms.

Simple Form	Simple Past Form	Simple Form	Simple Past Form
be	was/were	let	let
become	became	lose	lost
begin	began	make	made
break	broke	mean	meant
bring	brought	meet	met
buy	bought	pay	paid
choose	chose	put	put
come	came	read	read
cost	cost	ride	rode
do	did	run	ran
draw	drew	say	said
drink	drank	see	saw
drive	drove	set	set
eat	ate	sing	sang
feel	felt	speak	spoke
find	found	spend	spent
forget	forgot	stand	stood
get	got	take	took
give	gave	teach	taught
go	went	tell	told
have	had	think	thought
hear	heard	understand	understood
hit	hit	wake	woke
keep	kept	wear	wore
know	knew	write	wrote
leave	left		

1 **Fill in the blanks with the simple past form of the verb.**

Saturday ___was___ (*be*) a very busy day for Peter. He ___woke___ (*wake*) up at 7:00 A.M. He ___drank___ (*drink*) a glass of juice and ___ate___ (*eat*) a muffin quickly. Then he ___put___ (*put*) on his running shoes and ___ran___ (*run*) a mile because he wanted to get some exercise. He ___came___ (*come*) home and ___took___ (*take*) a shower. Finally, he ___left___ (*leave*) his house at 8:30 A.M.

He ___had___ (*have*) many things to do. He ___went___ (*go*) to the drugstore, picked up his dry cleaning, and ___met___ (*meet*) a friend for lunch. He ___got___ (*get*) home at 2:15 in the afternoon and ___wrote___ (*write*) a letter to his uncle.

2 **Practice with a partner. Take turns asking and answering questions about irregular verbs.**

Example: A: What does *brought* mean?
B: The past of *bring*.

Comparative Adjectives

The following chart explains spelling rules and when to use *-er* or *more* with comparative adjectives.

Spelling Rules	Examples
One-Syllable Adjectives Add *-er* to one-syllable adjectives. (If the adjective already ends in *-e*, add only an *r*.)	fast—faster cheap—cheaper large—larger
For one-syllable adjectives that end in a single vowel and a single consonant, double the consonant. Then add *-er*.	big—bigger thin—thinner slim—slimmer
Two-Syllable Adjectives For two-syllable adjectives that end in *-y*, change the *y* to *i* and add *-er*.	pretty—prettier ugly—uglier heavy—heavier
Other Adjectives with Two or More Syllables Use *more* with other adjectives that have two or more syllables.	useful—more useful beautiful—more beautiful dangerous—more dangerous expensive—more expensive
Irregular Adjectives These adjectives are irregular.	good—better bad—worse far—farther (distance)

1 Write the comparative form of each adjective.

1. fast _faster_
2. slow _slower_
3. big _bigger_
4. thin _thinner_
5. large _larger_
6. pretty _prettier_
7. heavy _heavier_
8. useful _more useful_
9. beautiful _more beautiful_
10. expensive _more expensive_
11. dangerous _more dangeros_
12. good _better_
13. bad _worse_
14. far _farther (distance)_

Superlative Adjectives

The following chart explains spelling rules and when to use *-est* or *the most* with superlative adjectives.

Spelling Rules	Examples
One-Syllable Adjectives Add *-est* to one-syllable adjectives. (If the adjective already ends in *-e*, add only *st*.)	fast—the fastest cheap—the cheapest large—the largest
For one-syllable adjectives that end in a single vowel and a single consonant, double the consonant. Then add *-est*.	big—the biggest thin—the thinnest slim—the slimmest
Two-Syllable Adjectives For two-syllable adjectives that end in *-y*, change the *y* to *i* and add *-est*.	pretty—the prettiest ugly—the ugliest heavy—the heaviest
Other Adjectives with Two or More Syllables Use *the most* with other adjectives that have two or more syllables.	useful—the most useful beautiful—the most beautiful dangerous—the most dangerous expensive—the most expensive
Irregular Adjectives These adjectives are irregular.	good—the best bad—the worst far—the farthest

1 Write the superlative form of each adjective.

1. fast _the fastest_

2. slow _____

3. big _____

4. thin _____

5. large _____

6. pretty _____

7. heavy _____

8. useful _____

9. beautiful _____

10. expensive _____

11. dangerous _____

12. good _____

13. bad _____

14. far _____

Two-Word Verbs

Here are some common two-word verbs. There are many more two-word verbs in English. New ones are being created all the time as the need arises. Many two-word verbs have more than one meaning. You may wish to add more two-word verbs to this list as you learn them.

Verb	Meaning	Example Sentence
call back	(telephone again)	Can I call you back in five minutes?
call off	(cancel)	I called the party off because I was sick.
call up	(telephone)	I called her up yesterday.
check out	(borrow from a library or office)	He checked out three books from the library.
clean up	(clean completely)	They cleaned up the kitchen after dinner.
find out	(learn something)	How did you find out her age?
give back	(return)	I'll give your book back tomorrow.
give up	(stop doing something)	He gave up smoking two weeks ago.
look up	(search for something in a book)	I looked the word up in the dictionary.
pick up	(go and get a person or thing)	I'll pick you up at 7 o'clock.
put on	(wear)	Put on a coat. It's cold outside.
put away	(put in the place where something is kept)	She put her clothes away.
turn down	(decrease the volume) OR (refuse a job offer)	Please turn the radio down. It's too loud. I turned down the job because the pay was too low.

turn off	(stop a machine)	Please turn off the TV.
turn on	(start a machine)	Please turn on the lights. It's dark in here.
turn up	(increase the volume)	Please turn the radio up. I can't hear it.
wake up	(make a person stop sleeping)	Please be quiet. You'll wake up the children.
write down	(make notes)	She wrote down the information.
_____	_____	_____
_____	_____	_____
_____	_____	_____
_____	_____	_____
_____	_____	_____
_____	_____	_____
_____	_____	_____
_____	_____	_____
_____	_____	_____
_____	_____	_____
_____	_____	_____
_____	_____	_____
_____	_____	_____
_____	_____	_____
_____	_____	_____

Past Participles (Irregular Verbs)

Here are some of the more common irregular verbs and their past participles. To form the present perfect, use **have** + the past participle of the main verb.

Simple Form	Past Participle	Simple Form	Past Participle
be	been	leave	left
become	become	let	let
begin	begun	lose	lost
break	broken	make	made
bring	brought	mean	meant
buy	bought	meet	met
choose	chosen	pay	paid
come	come	put	put
cost	cost	read	read
do	done	ride	ridden
draw	drawn	run	run
drink	drunk	say	said
drive	driven	see	seen
eat	eaten	set	set
feel	felt	sing	sung
find	found	speak	spoken
forget	forgotten	spend	spent
get	gotten	stand	stood
give	given	take	taken
go	gone	teach	taught
have	had	tell	told
hear	heard	think	thought
hit	hit	understand	understood
keep	kept	wear	worn
know	known	write	written

1 Write the past participle of these verbs.

1. be _been_

2. bring _____

3. do _____

4. drink _____

5. drive _____

6. forget _____

7. know _____

8. see _____

9. take _____

10. tell _____

11. think _____

12. write _____

Some Popular Names in the United States

First Names (Male)

Aaron	Jeremy
Adam	Jesse
Alan, Allen	John (Johnny)
Alexander (Alex)	Jonathan (Jon)
Andrew (Andy)	Joseph (Joe)
Anthony (Tony)	Keith
Benjamin (Ben)	Kenneth (Ken)
Brian, Bryan	Kevin
Carl	Lawrence (Larry)
Charles (Charlie, Chuck)	Mark, Marcus
Christopher (Chris)	Matthew (Matt)
Craig	Michael (Mike, Mitch)
Daniel (Dan, Danny)	Nicholas (Nick)
David (Dave)	Patrick (Pat)
Dennis	Paul
Derek (Derrick)	Peter (Pete)
Donald (Don)	Phillip, Philip (Phil)
Douglas (Doug)	Richard (Dick, Rich, Rick)
Edward (Ed)	Robert (Bob, Bobby, Rob)
Eric, Erik	Ronald (Ron)
Frank	Samuel (Sam)
Gabriel (Gabe)	Scott
Gary	Sean, Shawn, Shane
George	Stephen, Steven (Steve)
Gregory (Greg)	Taylor
Harold (Harry)	Thomas (Tom, Tommy)
Henry	Timothy (Tim)
James (Jim, Jimmy, Jamie, Jay)	Vincent (Vince)
Jason	William (Bill, Billy, Willie)
Jeffrey, Geoffrey (Jeff)	Zachary (Zach)

Alexandra
Alicia, Alice
Allison
Amanda
Amy
Angela
Anna, Ana, Ann, Anne
Betty
Bonnie
Carolyn, Caroline, Carolina (Carol, Carrie)
Catherine, Katherine (Cathy, Kathy, Kate, Katie)
Christine (Chris)
Cynthia (Cindy, Cindi)
Dawn
Deborah (Debbie)
Dorothy
Elizabeth (Beth, Betsy, Betty, Liz)
Emily
Erica
Frances (Fran)
Gina
Helen
Jacqueline (Jackie)
Jamie
Jane, Jean
Jennifer (Jenny)
Jessica
Julie, Julia
Karen
Kate, Katie

Kelly
Kimberly (Kim)
Kristen, Kristin (Kris)
Laura, Lauren
Leslie
Lisa
Louise
Margaret (Peggy)
Marie, Maria
Mary
Melinda (Linda)
Melissa
Michelle
Molly
Nancy
Natalie
Pamela (Pam)
Rachel
Rebecca (Becky)
Ruth
Samantha (Sam)
Sara, Sarah
Stacy, Stacey
Stephanie
Susan (Sue, Susie)
Tanya
Tiffany
Tina
Vanessa
Victoria

Last Names

The ten most common last names in the United States are:

Anderson
Brown
Davis
Johnson
Jones

Martin
Miller
Smith
Williams
Wilson

Other common American last names are:

Adams
Allen
Bell
Campbell
Carter
Clark
Coleman
Collins
Evans
Goldberg
González
Goodman
Gordon
Green, Greene
Griffin
Hall

Harris
Hill
Howard
Jackson
James
Kelly, Kelley
Kim
King
Lewis
Martin
Mitchell
Moore
Morris
Murphy
Nelson
Peterson
Robinson

Rodríguez
Ross
Sánchez
Scott
Sullivan
Taylor
Thomas
Thompson
Turner
Walker
Wang
Washington
White
Wright
Young

Sources

Bingwanger, Barbara, and Lisbeth Mah. *The Best Name for Your Baby*. New York: Henry, Holt and Company, 1990.

Dunkling, Leslie, and William Gosling. *The New American Dictionary of Baby Names*. New York: Signet, 1983.

Lansky, Bruce. *The Best Baby Name Book in the Whole Wide World*. New York: Meadowbrook, Inc., 1984.

United States Social Security Administration

The United States

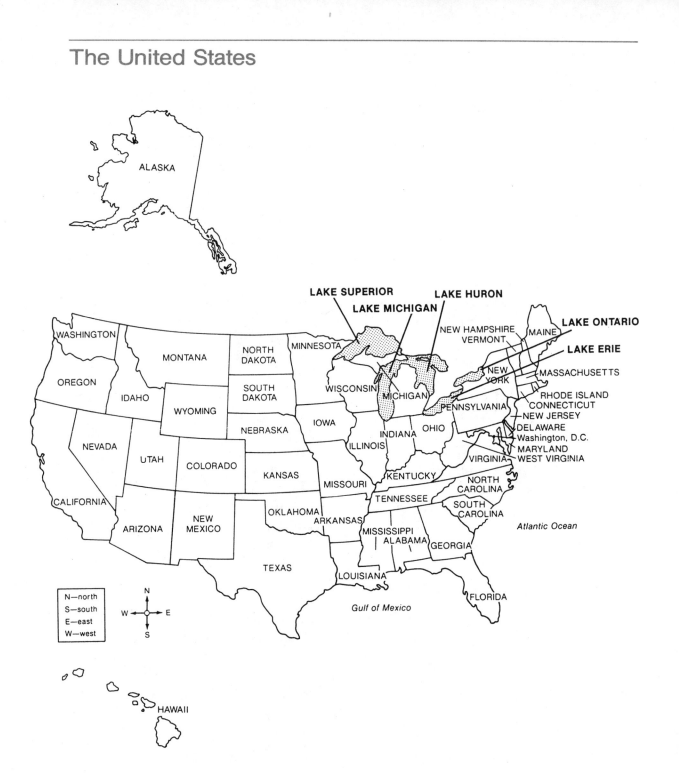

North America

Canada

NORTH AMERICA

United States of America

Mexico

Greenland

Iceland

Sw

No

United Kingdom

Denma

Ireland

Netherlands

Belgium

Luxembourg

France

Switzerland

Slo

Austria

EUROPE

Portugal

Spain

Albani

Tuni

Canada

NORTH AMERICA

United States of America

Morocco

Algeria

ATLANTIC OCEAN

Western Sahara

Mexico

Mauritania

Mali

Bahamas

Cuba

Dominican Republic

Jamaica

Puerto Rico

Belize

Haiti

Ni

Guatemala

Honduras

Dominica

Senegal

Burkina

El Salvador

Nicaragua

Barbados

The Gambia

Faso

Costa Rica

Trinidad and Tobago

Guinea-Bissau

Guinea

Nige

Panama

Venezuela

Guyana

Sierra Leone

Colombia

Suriname

Liberia

French Guiana

Ivory Coast

Equatorial

Ghana

Guinea

Ecuador

Togo

Benin

Peru

Sao Tome and Principe

SOUTH AMERICA

Brazil

Bolivia

Paraguay

Chile

Uruguay

Argentina

ARCTIC OCEAN

Russia

Estonia
Latvia
Lithuania
Poland
Belarus
The Czech Republic
Slovakia
Hungary Ukraine
Croatia
Romania
Serbia
Bulgaria
Macedonia
Turkey

Kazakhstan

Mongolia

North Korea

South Korea

Japan

Bosnia and Herzegovina
Georgia
Armenia
Turkmenistan
Azerbaijan
Afghanistan

Kyrgyzstan

Uzbekistan

ASIA

Tajikistan

China

Syria
Lebanon
Israel
Kuwait
Jordan
Bahrain
Qatar

Iraq

Iran

Pakistan

Nepal

Bhutan

Taiwan

PACIFIC OCEAN

India

Egypt

Saudi Arabia

United
Arab Emirates
Oman

Yemen

Bangladesh

Myanmar

Vietnam
Laos

Thailand

Chad

Sudan

Djibouti

Cambodia

Philippines

AFRICA

Ethiopia

Somalia

Central
African Republic

Sri Lanka

INDIAN OCEAN

Brunei
Malaysia
Singapore

Uganda
Kenya

Maldives

Solomon Islands

Zaire

Rwanda
Burundi

Tanzania

Seychelles

Indonesia

Papua New Guinea

Comoros

Angola

Malawi

Zambia

Zimbabwe

Madagascar

Mauritius

Botswana

Mozambique
Swaziland

Australia

Lesotho

South Africa

New Zealand

ANTARCTICA

Appendix

171

Answer Key

This section provides answers for written activities only. Because of the communicative nature of the oral activities, many of them will have varied answers. Some possible answers for these oral activities are included in the *English Connections Book 2 Teacher's Edition*.

Unit 1

Page 2
Exercise 1
Answers will vary.

1. I eat breakfast every day.
2. I read the newspaper every day.
3. I go to school every day.
4. I work every day.
5. I eat dinner every day.

Page 3
Exercise 3
1. NO
2. NO
3. YES
4. NO
5. NO

Exercise 4
Answers will vary.

1. I don't get up early.
2. I go shopping.
3. I don't go to work.
4. I clean my apartment.
5. I don't go to school.

Page 4
Exercises 6 and 7
Answers will vary.

Page 7
Exercise 11
Answers will vary. Here are some possible answers.

1. at 7 o'clock
2. at 7:30
3. at 6:30
4. about 10:00

Page 9
Exercise 15
1. 2
2. 4
3. 3
4. 1

Page 10
Exercise 16
1. He wakes up.
2. He shaves.
3. He gets dressed.
4. He goes to work.

Unit 2

Page 13
Exercise 3
1. Pablo is eating.
2. Tina and Juanita are reading.
3. Carlos is riding his bike.

Exercise 4
1. . . . feeding Pablo right now.
2. . . . vacuuming the apartment right now.
3. . . . washing the dishes right now. OR . . . doing the dishes right now.

Page 14
Exercise 6
1. The woman isn't doing the dishes. She's vacuuming.
2. The man isn't reading. He's fixing the lamp.
3. The baby isn't talking on the telephone. He's watching his mother.
4. The boy isn't watching TV. He's talking on the telephone.
5. The girls aren't studying. They're playing cards.
6. The cat isn't sleeping. It's eating.

Page 15
Exercise 7
1. No, he isn't. He's eating.
2. Yes, he is.
3. Yes, I am.
4. No, they aren't.

Page 18
Wrapping Up
Answers will vary. Here is one way:

   This is Carlos's birthday party. Carlos is seven years old. He is sitting near the birthday cake. His friend David is sitting near him. David is wearing his baseball hat again. And Tina is holding Pablo. Pablo is reaching for the cake. I am lighting the birthday candles.

Unit 3

Page 20
Exercise 1
1. A
2. B
3. B
4. A

Exercise 2
1. pounds
2. dishes
3. children
4. women

Page 21
Exercise 3
Count nouns: tomatoes, carrots, onions
Noncount nouns: cereal, sugar, rice

Exercise 4
Count nouns: tires, gas pumps, paper towels
Noncount nouns: air, gas, water, oil

Page 22
Exercise 5
Answers can be in any order.

1. a few tomatoes
2. a lot of milk
3. a lot of juice
4. a lot of eggs
5. a few onions
6. a little cheese

Exercise 6
Answers will vary.

Page 23
Exercise 8
Answers will vary.

Page 25
Exercise 11
Answers can be in any order.

1. two slices of bread
2. a bowl of cereal
3. a glass of milk
4. a glass of orange juice

Exercise 12
Answers will vary.

Page 26
Exercise 13
1. 1 lb.
2. 1 lb.
3. 1 qt.
4. 5 lbs.
5. ½ gal.
6. 1 pt.
7. 16 oz.
8. 1 gal.

Page 27
Exercise 14
Answers will vary.

Exercise 15
Answers will vary.

Page 28
Wrapping Up

Count Nouns
Singular—Plural
orange—oranges
teaspoon—teaspoons
dish—dishes
tire—tires
lemon—lemons
potato—potatoes
pound—pounds
child—children
man—men
tomato—tomatoes
woman—women

Noncount Nouns
sugar
salt
water
money
gas
oil
soup
juice
air

Review: Units 1–3

Pages 29–30
Exercise 2
Christmas in Mexico

1. Christmas and New Year's
2. Answers may vary. Here is one possible answer.
   They have parties. They have a lot of food and drinks. The night before New Year's Day everyone celebrates. They dance and drink. They eat tamales or turkey. At midnight they give thanks for the New Year.

The Moon Festival
1. the Moon Festival
2. Answers may vary. Here is one possible answer.
   They eat outside. They watch the full moon. Many people eat dinner outside. They eat mooncakes.

Unit 4

Page 32
Exercise 1
Answers will vary.

Page 33
Exercise 3
1. was, wasn't
2. wasn't, was
3. was, wasn't
4. weren't, were
Answer: Octavio

Exercise 4
Answers will vary.

Page 37
Exercise 9
1. at home
2. at work
3. at the video store

Exercise 10
Answers will vary.

Unit 5

Page 40
Exercise 1
1. A
2. B
3. B
4. A
5. B

Page 41
Exercise 2
1. She worked last Monday.
2. She cleaned her apartment last Tuesday.
3. She called her parents last Wednesday.
4. She walked three miles last Thursday.
5. She baked a cake last Friday.
6. She played with her children last Saturday.
7. She cooked a big meal last Sunday.

Exercise 3
1. found
2. ate
3. lost
4. heard
5. had
6. got

Page 42
Exercise 4
1. For *Maria. Mrs. Rogers* called.
   Message: *Please call her at 837-9045.*
2. For *Maria. Mrs. Gonzalez* called.
   Message: *She talked to Carlos and everything is fine.*

Exercise 5
1. She went to work.
2. She did the dishes.
3. She read the newspaper.
4. She did the grocery shopping.

Exercise 6
1. was born
2. started school
3. moved to San Juan
4. finished high school
5. got her first job
6. got married
7. had her first child
8. came to New York

Page 43
Exercise 9
1980—Puerto Rico
Maria didn't have any children. She went out to eat. She worked in an office.
1990—New York
Maria had three children. She ate at home. She didn't go out to eat. She wore glasses.

Exercise 10
Answers will vary.

Page 46
Exercise 14
1. 1969
2. 1783
3. 1876
4. 1850
5. 1861

Page 48
Exercise 17
1. c
2. a or b or e
3. a
4. b
5. d
6. Answers will vary.

Unit 6

Page 50
Exercise 1
Singular
There's a Laundromat on Franklin Street.
There's a shoe repair shop too.
There's an apartment building.
There's a small grocery store.
There's a bus stop.
There's a mailbox.

Plural

There are many buildings.

There are some cars.

There are some trees.

Page 52

Exercise 5

1. TRUE
2. TRUE
3. FALSE (There's a drugstore next to the bank.)
4. FALSE (There's a bank there.)
5. FALSE (There's a jewelry store across from the drugstore.)

Exercise 6

Answers may vary.

1. Yes, there is. It's across from the jewelry store.
2. Yes, there is. It's on the southwest corner of Main Street and Front Street.
3. Yes, there is. It's between the restaurant and the bookstore.
4. No, there isn't.
5. Yes, there is. It's on the northwest corner of Main Street and Front Street.
6. Yes, there is. It's on the northeast corner of Main Street and Front Street.

Page 53

Exercise 7

1. Rita lives on the first floor.
2. Ana lives on the second floor.
3. Peter lives on the third floor.
4. Victor lives on the fourth floor.
5. Ruth lives on the fifth floor.
6. Mark lives on the sixth floor.
7. Susan lives on the seventh floor.
8. Teresa lives on the eighth floor.
9. Abdul lives on the ninth floor.
10. Ivan lives on the tenth floor.

Page 54

Exercise 8

1. beauty school
2. first floor
3. second floor
4. travel agency
5. sixth floor
6. There's a copy shop on the second floor.
7. There's a construction company on the fourth floor.
8. There's a car rental company on the first floor.

Exercise 9

1. It's the first building on the left.
2. It's the second building on the right.
3. It's the third building on the right.
4. It's the third building on the left.
5. It's the fourth building on the left.
6. It's the fourth building on the right.

Page 55

Exercise 10

1. Excuse me. How do I get to *the bank*?
2. Excuse me. How do I get to *the drugstore*?
3. Excuse me. How do I get to *Central Hotel*?

Review: Units 4–6

Pages 59–60

Exercise 3

1. Mr. St. Fleur's second son was born.
2. Mr. St. Fleur drove his wife to the hospital.
3. He wore a hospital gown.
4. He cut the baby's umbilical cord.
5. He was very excited.
6. Answer depends on the current date.

Unit 7

Page 63

Exercise 3

Answers will vary.

1. A two-slice toaster is cheaper than an electric box fan.
2. A slimline phone is cheaper than an AM/FM stereo radio with cassette.
3. An electric box fan is cheaper than a slimline phone.
4. An AM/FM stereo radio is cheaper than an upright vacuum cleaner.
5. A boy's bike is cheaper than a color TV.
6. An AM/FM stereo radio is cheaper than a color TV.

Exercise 4

1. a pound of chicken
2. a quart of milk
3. a pound of margarine
4. a pound of oranges
5. a pound of carrots
6. a pound of rice

Page 64

Exercise 5

1. The large one.
2. The small one.
3. The large one.
4. The small one.

Exercise 6

Answers will vary.

1. Which car is cheaper, the Porsche or the convertible?
2. Which car is older, the station wagon or the sedan?
3. Which car is bigger, the van or the hatchback?

Page 65
Exercise 7
1. Parelli's Lasagna is more expensive. ($1.18/lb.)
2. Sunshine Juice Drinks are more expensive. ($0.66/qt.)
3. Chicken wings are more expensive. ($0.99/lb.)

Page 67
Exercise 13
The speaker is number 4.

Page 68
Use What You Know
Sentences will vary. Here are some possibilities:

1. sweet sweeter — Ice cream is sweeter than milk.
2. heavy heavier — Water is heavier than air.
3. small smaller — Sports cars are smaller than vans.
4. beautiful more beautiful — Mt. Hood is more beautiful than Mt. St. Helens.
5. big bigger — Vans are bigger than sports cars.
6. thin thinner — My sister is thinner than I am.
7. cold colder — Chicago is colder than Los Angeles in the winter.
8. tall taller — My brother is taller than I am.
9. useful more useful — Blenders are more useful than coffee makers.

Unit 8

Page 70
Exercise 1
Answers will vary.

1. I'm going to visit friends tomorrow.
2. I'm going to work tomorrow.
3. I'm going to plant some tomatoes tomorrow.
4. I'm going to clean my apartment tomorrow.

Page 71
Exercise 4
Answers may vary.

1. He's going to study.
2. He's going to play basketball.
3. He's going to eat a doughnut.

Page 72
Exercise 5
1. August 23, at 7 P.M.
2. Maria Sánchez
3. a birthday party
4. 23 Hanover Street, Apt. 3
5. comfortable clothes (Answers will vary.)
6. We're going to dance. (Answers will vary.)

Page 73
Answers will vary.

Page 75
Exercise 10
Answers will vary.

need to do
1. I need to go to the supermarket.
2. I need to do my laundry.
3. I need to pay my bills.
4. I need to register for a class.
want to do
1. I want to visit my sister.
2. I want to go to the beach.
3. I want to see a movie.
4. I want to take karate lessons.

Page 76
Wrapping Up
1. Hanh is going to watch the parade.
2. Magda is going to watch the parade with Hanh.
3. Thuy is going to be in the parade.
4. Chau is going to be in the parade.
5. Martin is going to watch the parade with his mother.

Unit 9

Page 78
Exercise 1
Adjective → Superlative
1. shy → the shyest
2. funny → the funniest
3. tall → the tallest
4. quiet → the quietest
5. young → the youngest
6. old → the oldest

Page 79
Exercise 4
1. Brazil
2. French Guiana
3. China
4. Luxembourg (Monaco, Andorra, and Vatican City are not on this map.)
5. Alaska
6. Rhode Island
7. Hawaii

Page 80
Exercise 6
Most expensive item first:
1. camera
2. lamp
3. hair dryer
4. flashlight

Page 82

Exercise 8

Jules is the last person on the right.

Exercise 9

1. Who's the tallest person in the class?
2. Whose book is on your desk?
3. Whose pencil is this?
4. Who's your best friend?
5. Who's sitting on your right?
6. Whose grandmother is this?

Page 83

Exercise 10

Answers will vary.

1. I hate washing the floor.
2. I hate ironing.
3. I hate cooking.
4. I hate doing the dishes.

Page 84

Wrapping Up

1. young   the youngest
2. tall   the tallest
3. shy   the shyest
4. quiet   the quietest
5. funny   the funniest
6. old   the oldest
7. short   the shortest
8. outgoing   the most outgoing
9. talkative   the most talkative
10. serious   the most serious

Review: Units 7–9

Pages 85–86

Exercise 3

Washington

Exercise 4

Maine

Exercise 5

largest to smallest: Texas, Florida, South Carolina, Maryland, Rhode Island

Exercise 6

five

largest to smallest: Lake Superior, Lake Michigan, Lake Huron, Lake Erie, Lake Ontario

Exercise 7

Florida, Georgia, South Carolina, North Carolina, Virginia, Maryland, Delaware, New Jersey, New York

---

Unit 10

Page 88

Exercise 1

Answers will vary. Here are some possible answers.

1. I have to cook dinner.
2. I have to work.
3. I have to fix my car.
4. I have to go to the dentist.
5. I have to do my laundry.
6. I have to write a letter.

Page 90

Exercise 7

1. Ramón   NO
2. François   YES
3. Nam   NO
4. Hanh   YES

Page 91

Exercise 8

1. Maria <u>can't</u> go.
2. Hanh <u>can't</u> go.
3. Magda <u>can't</u> go.
4. Rita's brother <u>can</u> go.

Exercise 9

1. very busy
2. very sad
3. very tired (sleepy)
4. very funny
5. Answers will vary.

Page 92

Exercise 10

1. A
2. B
3. B
4. A
5. A
6. B

Exercise 11

Answers will vary.

1. Maria can speak Spanish.
2. Ramón can drive a delivery truck.
3. Hanh can't speak Spanish.
4. Nam can speak Vietnamese.
5. Magda can speak Russian.
6. Martin can't drive.

Page 93

Exercise 12

Answers will vary.

1. An artist can draw pictures.
2. A TV comedian can make people laugh.
3. A taxi driver can drive you where you need to go.
4. A tailor or a seamstress can sew well.

Page 95
Exercise 16
Answers may vary.

Unit 11

Page 98
Exercise 1
1. A
2. B
3. B
4. A
5. A
6. B

Page 99
Exercise 2
Answers will vary.

Exercise 3
Answers will vary.

Exercise 4
Answers will vary.

1. She will pick him up.
2. She will answer the phone.
3. She will give him some Tylenol for his headache.

Page 100
Exercise 5
Answers will vary.

1. I won't be late.
2. I won't lose it.
3. I won't ride in the street.
4. I won't drop it.

Page 101
Exercise 7
Answers will vary.

1. It will take 10 minutes to shave.
2. It will take 45 minutes to get a haircut.
3. It will take an hour to read the newspaper.
4. It will take an hour to wash the car.
5. It will take an hour and a half to buy groceries for a week.

Exercise 8
Answers will vary.

1. Maria wants to visit her mother in Puerto Rico.
   Question: How will Maria go there?
   Prediction: She'll go there by plane.
2. Ramón hopes to buy a new car.
   Question: How much will it cost?
   Prediction: It'll cost about $10,000.00.

Page 102
Exercise 9
1. Present
2. Future
3. Present
4. Future
5. Past

Exercise 10
1. She's planning a trip.
2. No, she didn't call her.
3. She'll call her in a minute.

Exercise 11
1. Where are you going, Rita?
2. Did you get a passport photo?
3. Are we going to meet at the restaurant?

Page 103
Exercise 12
Answers will vary.

1. I plan to take a trip next year.
2. I plan to move next month.
3. I plan to get a full-time job in a few years.
4. I plan to buy a winter coat in a few weeks.
5. I plan to get married next year.
6. I plan to get a haircut next week.

Unit 12

Page 106
Exercise 1
Answers may vary.

1. It might be a picture.
2. It might be a record.
3. It might be a mirror.
4. It might be some earrings.
5. It might be a watch.
6. It might be a pen-and-pencil set.

Page 107
Exercise 2
Answers will vary.

1. She might be at home during a power outage.
   She might be in a movie theater.
   She might be in her living room. She might be watching a movie on TV.
2. He might be at the YMCA.
   He might be at school.
   He might be at his friend's house.
3. He might be at a Vietnamese restaurant.
   He might be at his mother's house.
   He might be at his friend's house.

Exercise 3
Answers will vary.

1. It might be a spoon.
   It might also be a bottle.
   It might be a broken bell.
   It might be a stomach.
   It might be a balloon with the top cut off.
2. It might be a bird flying over the water.
   It might be a ball bouncing in the air.
   It might be a rock over the water.
3. It might be a fishing rod with a rock on the end of it.
   It might be a yo-yo hanging from the ceiling.

Exercise 4
1. might
2. will
3. might
4. will

Page 109
Exercise 5
1. Tina is too sick.
2. Maria is too tired.
3. Ramón is too busy.

Exercise 7
1. too
2. very
3. very
4. too

Page 110
Exercise 8
1. Fred can't get a driver's license because he's not old enough.
2. Mr. Johnson can't get out of bed because he's not strong enough.
3. Pablo can't play in the pool because the water's not warm enough.
4. Laura can't cut the meat because the knife is not sharp enough.

Exercise 9
Answers may vary.

1. I can't cut this paper. The scissors are <u>not sharp enough</u>.
2. I can't sit in this chair. It's <u>not strong enough</u>.
3. No, I'm not. It's <u>not clean enough</u>.
4. I don't think so. The water is <u>not warm enough</u>.
5. No, I didn't. It wasn't <u>big enough/good enough/fast enough</u>.

Page 111
Exercise 10
1. too
2. very
3. enough
4. too
5. very

Review: Units 10–12
Pages 113–114
Exercise 1
1. People have to wear shoes.
2. The store opens at 10 A.M. on Tuesday.
3. No, you can't.
4. It closes at 9 P.M. on Friday.
5. You can't eat, drink, or smoke.
6. Yes, you can pay with MasterCard or Visa.

Exercise 3
Answers will vary.

1. day-care center
2. record/CD store
3. bakery
4. stationery store
5. day-care center
6. restaurant/travel agency
7. hair salon
8. frame shop

Exercise 4
1. You have to use quarters.
2. You have to wear a shirt.
3. You cannot park here.
4. You can use this door in an emergency.

Exercise 5
Answers may vary. Here are some possible answers.

1. An alarm will ring.
2. She might get a parking ticket.
3. He might say, "You can't eat here. You have to wear shoes."

Unit 13
Pages 116–117
Exercise 1
1. Watch out!
2. Hurry up!
3. Be careful! OR Watch out!
4. Watch out!
5. Take two slices of bread. . . .

Page 118
Exercise 2
Answers will vary.

1. Please put away your things.
   Don't leave your jacket in the living room.
2. Please be quiet.
   Don't make so much noise.
3. Please wait for dinner.
   Please don't eat now.
4. Turn off the TV and go to bed.
   Don't stay up late.

iet?

oke?

dow.

the window?

atient.

me with this patient?

ase open the door for me?

uld you please open the door for me?

Page 119
Exercise 4
1. b
2. a
3. d
4. c
5. f
6. e

Exercise 5
Answers may vary.

1. OK.
2. Of course.
3. Of course.
4. Sure.

Page 120
Exercise 6
1. Oh, I'll turn down the radio.
2. I'll turn up the TV.
3. I'll turn on the radio.
4. I'll turn off the TV.

Exercise 7
1. d
2. c
3. a
4. b

Page 121
Exercise 8
A: Would you please <u>clean up</u> the living room? It's a mess! Some <u>friends</u> are coming over after the baseball game.

B: Oh, when will the game start?

A: I'm not sure. Let's <u>call up</u> the coach and <u>find out</u>. (*calling him up*) Oh. His line is busy. We'll have to <u>call back</u> later.

B: Well, they might <u>call off</u> the game because it's starting to rain now.

A: I hope they don't. Do we have enough sacks for the party?

B: I think so. But don't serve any potato chips. Irene is trying to <u>give up</u> junk food because she wants to lose weight.

A: Don't worry. I won't. Don't forget to <u>give back</u> the CDs we borrowed after the party.

B: I won't.

Page 122
Exercise 9
1. A: give back
   B: it
2. A: put away
   B: them
3. A: turn off
   B: it
4. A: turn on
   B: them
5. A: turn down
   B: it
6. A: pick me up
   B: you

Unit 14

Page 127
Exercise 2
Answers will vary.

1. She should try to become a manager in a clothing store.
2. She should visit a lot of dress shops.

Page 129
Exercise 7
Answers will vary. Here are some possible answers.

1. He should take a Spanish class.
2. He should join a club. He should take a class.
3. She should get a nicotine patch.
4. She should try to make some new friends.

Page 130
Exercise 9
Answers will vary.

1. Library:
   You should talk softly./You shouldn't talk loudly.
   You shouldn't eat or drink there.
2. Movie theater:
   You shouldn't talk loudly.
   You shouldn't wear hats.
   You shouldn't bring babies.
3. Gas station:
   You shouldn't smoke.
   You should turn off your engine.

Exercise 10
Answers will vary.

1. You should both compromise. One weekend you should go out. The next weekend you should stay home.
2. You should talk to her about this.
3. You should talk to friends about this. You should look in the ad section of the newspaper.

Page 131

Exercise 11

1. Oh, you'd better see a dentist.
2. You'd better stay home today.
3. She'd better go to the doctor.

Page 132

Exercise 12

Answers will vary.

1. stay in bed/take some Tylenol/get some rest
2. stay in bed/get some rest/see a doctor
3. take it now
4. make one now

Unit 15

Page 137

Exercise 3

A: Have you <u>ever</u> worked in a restaurant?
B: Yes, I have. I worked at The Happy Wok restaurant <u>from</u> 1990 <u>to</u> 1993. I also worked at a restaurant <u>in</u> my country six years <u>ago</u>.
A: Are you working now?
B: No. I left my job <u>last</u> year because I wanted to study full time.
A: Have you finished your studies?
B: Yes, I have. I graduated two weeks <u>ago</u>.

Page 139

Exercise 8

1. fill out
2. look over
3. fill out
4. turn . . . down
5. call up

Page 140

Exercise 9

Police Officer:
1. True
2. False
3. False
4. True

Teacher:
1. True
2. False
3. False

Post Office Employee:
1. True
2. False
3. False
4. True
5. False

Page 141

Exercise 11

1. You must not drive faster than the
2. You must not enter here.
3. You must not pass any cars here.
4. You must drive only in the direction of t arrow.
5. You must not turn right or left on a red ligh
6. You must not make a U-turn here.

Exercise 12

1. must not
2. don't have to
3. must not
4. don't have to
5. must not
6. don't have to
7. must not
8. don't have to
9. don't have to
10. don't have to

Page 142

Exercise 14

1. Yes, she has.
2. Two years ago.
3. She decided to go back to school.

Review: Units 13–15

Pages 143–144

Exercise 1

1. False
2. True
3. True
4. False
5. False
6. True

Appendix

Spelling of Simple Present
Page 148

Mae-Ning <u>wants</u> to be a computer programmer. She <u>goes</u> to Portland Community College. She <u>has</u> classes four nights a week. She <u>likes</u> her classes, and she <u>studies</u> very hard.

She <u>has</u> a full-time job during the day. She <u>works</u> at a preschool. She <u>teaches</u> the children songs, and she <u>plays</u> with them.

She <u>likes</u> her busy schedule.

Spelling of -*ing* Forms
Page 149

1. Ramón is very busy in the morning. Right now he <u>is getting</u> ready for work. He <u>is shaving</u>. He <u>is trying</u> to get to work on time.

ry busy in the evening. ...ooking dinner. She is ...ert. Her baby is sitting ...s crying. Tina and ...homework. Carlos is ...andmother. Ramón is ...e table.

3. cake—1
4. father—2
5. grandfather—3
6. lunch—1
7. sisters—2
8. pineapple—3

Pronunciation of Plural Nouns
Page 153
Exercise 2
1. no extra syllable
2. no extra syllable
3. extra syllable
4. extra syllable
5. no extra syllable
6. extra syllable
7. no extra syllable
8. no extra syllable
9. extra syllable

Spelling of Plural Nouns
Page 154
Exercise 1
1. roses
2. tables
3. toys
4. houses
5. men
6. people
7. ladies
8. knives
9. classes
10. tomatoes
11. mice
12. women
13. children
14. strawberries

Pronunciation of the Simple Past
Page 157
Exercise 2
1. no extra syllable
2. no extra syllable
3. extra syllable
4. no extra syllable
5. extra syllable
6. no extra syllable
7. no extra syllable
8. extra syllable
9. extra syllable

Simple Past (Irregular Verbs)
Page 159
Saturday was a very busy day for Peter. He woke up at 7:00 A.M. He drank a glass of juice and ate a muffin quickly. Then he put on his running shoes and ran a mile because he wanted to get some exercise. He came home and took a shower. Finally, he left his house at 8:30 A.M.

He had many things to do. He went to the drugstore, picked up his dry cleaning, and met a friend for lunch. He got home at 2:15 in the afternoon and wrote a letter to his uncle.

Comparative Adjectives
Page 160
Exercise 1
1. faster
2. slower
3. bigger
4. thinner
5. larger
6. prettier
7. heavier
8. more useful
9. more beautiful
10. more expensive
11. more dangerous
12. better
13. worse
14. farther

Superlative Adjectives
Page 161
Exercise 1
1. the fastest
2. the slowest
3. the biggest
4. the thinnest
5. the largest
6. the prettiest
7. the heaviest
8. the most useful
9. the most beautiful
10. the most expensive
11. the most dangerous
12. the best
13. the worst
14. the farthest

Past Participles (Irregular Verbs)
Page 164
Exercise 1
1. been
2. brought
3. done
4. drunk
5. driven
6. forgotten
7. known
8. seen
9. taken
10. told
11. thought
12. written